Antique British Clocks
A Buyer's Guide

Antique British Clocks
A Buyer's Guide

Brian Loomes

ROBERT HALE · LONDON

ISBN 0 7090 4611 1

Robert Hale Limited
Clerkenwell House
Clerkenwell Green
London EC1R 0HT

Drawings entitled 'Representative parts and styles on a clock dial'
and 'Terms used in describing casework' were drawn by David Barker
and originally appeared in *Grandfather Clocks and their Cases*
published by David & Charles Ltd.

Set in Palatino by
Derek Doyle & Associates, Mold, Clwyd.
Printed in Great Britain by
St Edmundsbury Press, Bury St Edmunds, Suffolk.
Bound by WBC Bookbinders Ltd.

Contents

The photographs in this book are almost entirely of clocks the author has handled as a dealer over the years. The photographs were taken by the author and his son Robert. They were processed and printed by the author's wife Joy and his son.

Foreword

This book sets out to answer all the questions a beginner might wish to ask, if only he could think of them all. I have been a dealer in antique clocks for twenty-five years. In that time I have attempted to answer every question asked by every potential customer to the best of my ability. There were a lot of them and some defeated me. It occurred to me what a lot of breath I might save if it were possible to condense all these questions and answers into a single book, for no existing book approaches the subject from that point of view. This is the result. I hope it will help you as much as I hope it will help me.

Brian Loomes
Pateley Bridge, North Yorks, 1991

Introduction

The purpose of this book is to assist anyone wanting to buy an antique British clock, and especially a potential buyer with little or no experience. Such a person might find the subject fascinating and the first purchase might be one of many. Initially, however, the buyer is looking to buy a single clock, and first-time buyers will usually be thinking in terms of a longcase clock, if for no other reason than that other types of British clock tend to be a bit more of an acquired taste. Few first-time buyers would start off with a bracket clock, fewer still with a lantern clock, though a spring-driven wall clock is a possibility.

The beginner who looks at a few clocks may well find himself bemused, and this is hardly surprising since he has little concept of what he is looking at and cannot begin to understand prices and values. So he needs a little assistance, in fact probably a lot of assistance, which is hopefully what this book will provide. At the same time, however, he may not want to become a student of clocks, to learn about styles and ages, and periods and principles of movements. It all sounds so complicated. He does not want to get into all that gearing and mechanics, and who can blame him? Engineers revel in such things, but he's not an engineer and doesn't want to be one. All he wants to do is buy a clock, just one clock, and a few hints and tips on what to look for are probably all that he feels are necessary.

Well, a few hints and tips are easily provided and any reader can dip into this book here and there without having to read it from cover to cover. Clocks are a very easy subject and really quite interesting. The bit the reader really wants to know about, however, is the hard bit: how much should I have to pay? how can I pick up a bargain? how can I avoid paying over the odds? how do I recognize a 'good' clock? is it genuine or fake? will it be an investment? There is an answer to all these questions, but those answers may not be understood by a reader who knows nothing about the subject. You can hardly understand the value of a clock unless you know something about it, so the would-be buyer is going to have to consider various factors such as age, style, shape, size, colour and condition, though not necessarily in great detail. On the other hand, he may well find that once he begins to learn a little about clocks, the fever will grip him and he will want to know more.

The first question you should ask yourself before you buy a clock is: why are you buying it? Do you want a genuine antique clock, unaltered since the day it was made apart from cleaning and repairing, one with its original movement and in its original case, one that the clockmaker could recognize, if he could see it, as being exactly the same object he sold two hundred or more years ago? If you buy such a clock then a considerable part of the pleasure of owning it is in knowing that you have something genuine and real, something that has not been altered, modified, modernized or butchered for whatever reason. Such clocks do exist and they don't necessarily cost the earth. I am a clock dealer and I am searching for such clocks all day and every day, but in that search I have to reject as many as nine out of every ten that I come across, either because they do not fulfil those conditions, or because some other factor convinces me that I don't want to put my money into them.

Those other off-putting factors are very important and numerous and we shall examine them in some detail later. My very briefly summarized attitude is as follows. I don't want a clock if it is not genuine. It must not be too big or in bad condition, mechanically or casewise, though mechanical problems can very often be resolved – we can usually mend the engine if the bodywork is good. It must not be of an ugly style or bad colour. It should be of a reasonable age, which, for me personally, means no newer than about 1850. It must not have anything about it which puts it into the category of being a bad seller. Finally, it must not be so expensive that it prices itself out of its own market. Most of these are purely commercial considerations, but many of them will be, or ought to be, uppermost in the mind of the first-time buyer too. Unfortunately at this stage the novice does not know how to evaluate such commercial points. How big is too big? What constitutes ugliness? What is meant by good condition? What is bad colour? We shall come to all these points in due course.

First, however, let us consider the great percentage of clocks which are not genuine. These fall into many categories. There can be genuine clocks in non-genuine cases, dials in original cases but with non-original movements, clocks made up from old bits and pieces by an amateur bodger or professional faker, old clocks in new cases, old cases with new clocks in, old clocks with a modern electric movement, old cases with dials and no movement, cases

Twelve-inch dial of the eight-day clock by John Fladgate of London. This is a typical London clock.

Eight-day all-mahogany clock of about 1760 by John Fladgate of London, standing only about 7 ft. 5 in. Plus points: original double plinth to case, small height (for London), fine flame figuring to door and bookmatching to base.

without clocks in them, movements without dials, dials without movements. You do not need to attend many auctions to come across some clocks that fall into one of these categories, and sooner or later a buyer is found for all of them.

Many will appear to be bargains. Some buyers will purchase such clocks unaware that they are buying a 'wrong 'un', but others will buy them knowing full well what they have bought. Some of these clocks may have been altered many years ago, and some were altered recently to deceive naïve buyers deliberately. There are people who make a living making up fakes to sell to the gullible! Some people convince themselves that an old alteration somehow does not count as an alteration. Some would not mind if a clock was put into a different case 100 years ago, but would mind if it was done last week. Consequently, to oblige them, those who put clocks into different cases today make it look as if it was done 100 years ago. In the end, an alteration is still an alteration.

The buyer who is fussy about what he buys, as I am, is going to have a much harder time to buy anything at all, than someone who does not really care about genuineness. That is perfectly obvious. Much more of my time is spent examining and rejecting clocks I don't want than clocks I do want. For some buyers, genuiness is not particularly important. They may want to buy an old clock for reasons which, in their minds, do not demand genuineness. For instance they may want to buy an old clock to stand in the hall where some other object previously stood, one to match the colour of the panelling, one with a dial colour to match the curtains, one to look the part without working as they can't stand the noise of it ticking. Many more are quite happy with a clock that is old, or partly old, that shows the time and strikes the hours, that they like the look of and they are not really concerned how genuine or how old it might be. Such a clock is known as a 'furnishing-piece', which describes a clock which is not genuine, but looks nice in its own way. And for these kinds of buyers there is no earthly point in paying the price of the genuine article, because they can buy something to meet their particular needs at a much lower price.

Buyers are quite at liberty to take that attitude and many do, and there is no shame in it. This point of view would not suit a purist 'collector', but even the most fastidious collector will bend the rules when it suits him. Take for instance the situation where a clock comes along which is of a very rare or unusual nature, by a particularly special maker or something he is unlikely ever to see the like of again, but it is not in the original case. Does he pass it by as not genuine, or does he accept that in this instance he will

Eight-day all-mahogany longcase by Robert
Croal of Alyth, Scotland, *circa* 1850–60.
English-made dial with typical Victorian
landscapes. Of small size (6 ft. 11 in.) and in
very clean condition. Plus points: small stature,
all-mahogany construction, well-shaped trunk
quarter-columns and hood pillars to match.

buy it, even though not in its original case? Well, by and large he will accept it. For instance, how many clocks by Fromanteel, maker of the very first British pendulum clocks, are in their original cases? Would the fact that they may not be stop a collector from buying one? I have, in fact, bought clocks that came into this category (though not by Fromanteel), which I would never get a second chance of purchasing. So if rules may be bent sometimes, the question of when becomes one of value judgement, a matter of opinion, and that opinion is only as valid as the experience of the person holding it. What might seem like a rare and never-to-be-seen-again treasure of a clock to one person may be commonplace to someone with greater experience.

And what about the many clocks which have lost their cases, perhaps destroyed by woodworm or fire? What if you came across a clock movement and dial by Fromanteel tomorrow with no case? Would you buy it or turn it away? I would recommend you to buy it, if you could afford it. What would one do, however if it was a clock by a little-known maker? Do we save the best and leave the rest for the scrapheap? If so, who decides which are the best? It often happens that a movement turns up without a case – in an outhouse or a loft for instance – because metal movements are more durable than wooden cases. The owner must then decide to either make a new case or try to find a suitable old one, if he wants to preserve the clock. So, clocks do end up in wrong cases all the time, and sometimes for quite honourable reasons.

Where the whole question of whether or not to accept a clock, that is not entirely original, gets into difficulty, is when the buyer *thinks* he is buying the genuine item but, in fact, is not. Actually, very few people set out to buy a clock *intending* to buy one that is not genuine. It follows that if they do buy a furnishing-piece, they do so by mischance or because they have been deceived. If they knew it was wrong, they might still be tempted to buy it because they thought it was cheap. Often they are paying the full price, however, or think they are, and are still getting a furnishing-piece, or a 'marriage' as it is often called, being a clock consisting of parts that are not original to each other.

I'll always remember a situation which occurred some years ago. Someone I had met by chance on several occasions, and with whom I had many an interesting chat, was a keen, although modest, collector of antiques. He had spoken to me several times about his longcase clock. Then, the day which I had been dreading finally arrived. My wife and I were asked to dinner by this very pleasant couple, but all the way through the meal I knew what was going to happen. I was eventually invited to have a look at the clock. The reality of it was even worse than I had imagined.

Oak clock with mahogany trim by Thomas Armstrong of Hawkshead, *circa* 1790 standing about 6 ft. 11 in. Plus points of the case: very small in height, clean condition, good shape to swan neck.

It was the most appalling 'marriage' of a much altered brass-dial clock in a totally wrong case. The owner told me how long he had had it, who he had bought it from (a dealer I knew well, in fact), how much he had paid for it, and wanted me to confirm that it was a good buy and a good investment.

I simply agreed with him and left him happy in his ignorance. I just had not the heart to spoil the pleasure he obviously took from it, nor to risk embarrassing him in front of his wife by explaining that he had bought a pile of junk. I was only relieved that he was not hoping to sell it to me! Next time I saw that particular dealer I mentioned that I had been to dinner at so-and-so's, and had been shown the clock that he bought from him some years before because I could not resist watching him squirm. I also hinted that so-and-so was wondering about selling the clock and might be giving the dealer a ring shortly!

That is perhaps the biggest problem with furnishing-pieces. They are fine when you are buying them, but wait until you try to sell them. Of course, you might then be fortunate to find a buyer who either doesn't care or doesn't know whether it is genuine.

Recently I had a letter from someone who had been reading one of my books and took me to task for my attitude about furnishing-pieces. He pointed out that he had bought his longcase, of which he sent me a photograph, some ten years or more ago at a local auction, and he had enjoyed ten years of pleasurable ownership, until recently when he examined it more carefully in the light of my book and found it was in a non-original case, a marriage in fact. This had come as a surprise to him, but in the end it didn't really matter, he pointed out, because he liked the clock anyway. He thought it was a shame to get rid of it because it was not entirely genuine.

I could only point out in reply that when he bought the clock at £300, he bought it thinking it was genuine and at a bargain price. If he had been less keen to get a bargain, and had paid £350, he could have bought a genuine one which would have given him just as much pleasure, would have stood up to the closest scrutiny later, and if the time ever came when he wanted to sell it, it could not have been faulted by the buyer. It is surprising how often owners who discover much too late that they have bought a 'marriage' console themselves by announcing that it does not really matter because they like it anyway.

The main point about genuineness from a buyer's point of view is to ask yourself whether or not it is important for you to buy a genuine clock, or whether you will be just as happy with a furnishing-piece, which *should* come cheaper. If you want to buy a £2,000 clock, then you are not going to be able to buy it for £1,000

Ten-inch dial of early single-handed clock, *circa* 1720, by Robert Henderson of Scarborough. Note blank corners are typical of some Quaker work. Plus points: early period, respected maker, crisp engraving.

unless it is a 'marriage' of some sort. You will find that it is very easy to distinguish one from the other and there is a whole chapter later in this book on how to do precisely that.

For some buyers, many in fact, the reason for buying an antique clock is much the same as for buying any other antique, being principally for the pleasure of owning such an item. Some buyers, however, even within this category, have other reasons for making a purchase. Will it be an investment or a hedge against inflation? The answer to both questions is that in all probability it will. That has certainly been the case in the past, as the value of antique clocks today stands vastly ahead of inflation in relation to say twenty years ago, or even ten.

If you think you can buy an antique clock today and sell it for a profit next year or the year after, you will probably find that you are sadly mistaken. In the longer term, however, you may find that you can make a profit. On the other hand, a great deal depends on what you pay. Recently, a dealer told me about a fusee wall clock he had seen in a shop priced at £2,500. It is well-known in the trade that a good example of such a clock can be seen on sale every day of the week in dozens of shops for about £600 or £700. This was simply a case of a dealer trying it on, and if he ever does sell it to some unfortunate victim, the buyer will never get his money back on it. If a buyer shops around a bit, as most do, he will soon realize that that particular clock is vastly over-priced, so the chances are it will sit there for years without selling.

There are some buyers, not many fortunately, who see antiques purely as alternative investments, with the advantage that they may be tax free. If you are one, then I would strongly urge you to invest in some other financial gamble. Go take the advice of your bank manager and then you will have someone to grumble at when the Stock Exchange takes its next tumble.

The position on Capital Gains Tax at the time of writing is, I am advised, that if a private person sells one or more antique clocks (or any other item for that matter) up to a total annual value of less than £5,000, he need not disclose these on his tax declaration. If such sales exceed £5,000 in any one year, he is obliged to disclose them, but the first £4,000 of 'profit' is allowed tax-free, and the profit is calculated after a varying annual figure is allowed to cover inflation (deflation of money values). For a private owner these terms seem to be very reasonable. Anyone making a habit of such practice, however, might well be regarded, for tax purposes, as a dealer in those items, and the line between a 'collector' changing an item or two in his collection, and a commercial trader is a fine one to tread.

No doubt, when you begin your search you will have in mind the type of clock you feel you would like – provided you can see one you like at a price you can afford. Many will see a longcase clock as their first, or even their only, purchase. If that is the case, then do not try to take in too much at once. Read about longcase clocks and nothing else, because if you try to assimilate the styles of bracket, lantern, fusee and tavern clocks all at once, you may end up in a spin. The great majority of longcase clocks you will come across in your search will date roughly in the last hundred years of longcase clockmaking, say 1770–1870, and most will be white dials. Yet, most books have to begin at the beginning, namely over a hundred years earlier. If you want to buy a white-dial clock, there is no point in getting deeply into brass-dial styles, as they will not apply. By all means read the whole story, but concentrate on those aspects of importance to you, so that you can acquire some defined parameters on which to base your choice.

As much as ninety-five per cent of all British antique clocks one meets with today are longcase examples: those made before 1870, that is. After this date most clocks sold here were imported from Germany, America or France, even though they might carry the name of an English retailer. For that reason, this book concentrates to a large extent on longcases. As it happens, longcases are probably easier to understand than any other type, especially for a beginner. It is also fortunate that, once the styles of longcase clocks are understood, the styles of other types are so much easier to recognize.

1 Dials: Style, Age and Quality

The dial is the part of the clock that you see. A good one will be a pleasure to look at for ever. In the end what really matters is what you as the buyer find pleasing, regardless of what anyone else might or might not like and regardless of whether it is a good one in commercial or collecting terms.

It may help you, however, if you know how to recognize a good dial and how the dial itself will help to tell you the age of the clock. Such things have an important bearing on the value, which is something you are probably greatly concerned with.

Longcase clocks are the easiest of all British clocks to understand in terms of style and age. Understanding the style will help you to assess how old it is, and when you can date a longcase you are well on the way towards dating any other kind of British antique clock. The clock dial can tell you an amazing amount about the clock, provided you understand what you are looking at.

Longcase clocks were made for roughly two hundred years, from about 1660 to 1860. During that time, their style changed in a simple and consistent manner, which is very easy to understand, but, of course, with numerous and complicated variations on the theme, which may at first seem totally baffling to a novice. Let's look at the simplest elements first. The oldest clocks were small and slim and the newest of them tall and wide. The transition from one to the other is the story of the history of clock styles reduced to its simplest elements.

The very first longcases were made in 1658, but you and I are unlikely ever to see one on the market that was made before 1680. Everything involved in a clock's style begins with the dial. The early dials were small and the later ones large. How small? Well, some very early longcases may have dials as small as eight or nine inches square, but by 1680 anything less than ten inches square was unusual. At the other end of the time scale the largest dials might reach twice that, at a maximum of say sixteen inches, but such massive dials were very unusual and fifteen inches is the biggest dial one is likely to come across.

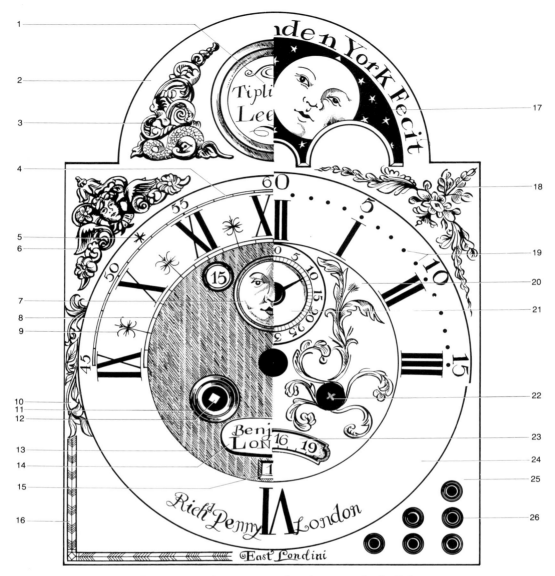

Representative parts and styles on a clock dial

1. Name boss in arch	15 Calendar of square box type
2 Dial arch	16 Herringbone (or wheatear) engraved
3 Arch spandrel	decoration
4 Minute band	17 Moon dial (rolling moon)
5 Half-quarter marker	18 Engraved corner decoration
6 Corner spandrel	19 Dotted minutes
7 Penny-moon dial	20 Engraved dial centre
8 Quarter-hour marker	21 Seconds dial
9 Half-hour marker	22 Winding arbor or winding square
10 Engraving between spandrels	(leaf-shaped here)
11 Ringed winding-hole	23 Curved date aperture or mouth
12 Plain winding-square	calendar
13 Matted dial centre (striped here, but	24 Chapter ring
often random)	25 Dial sheet
14 Nameplate	26 Cup-and-ring turned decoration

Dial sizes are measured in width, by the way, corner to corner along the bottom edge of the dial plate. Sizing by width avoids the problem that some are square and some are arched. Round dials are measured across their diameter. The growth in dial size from 1680 to 1860 was gradual and subject to variation in different regions and also depended upon the whims of different customers. Any attempt at summarizing this change must obviously be an imprecise art, but dial size is such a useful factor that, with one or two other facts thrown in, this alone can be almost sufficient to date and even help price a clock.

The earliest dials were made of brass. Painted dials (at the time called white dials) were introduced about 1770 and by the end of the century had ousted the brass dial completely from fashion. So we have roughly a hundred years of brass dial-making and a hundred years of painted dials; the two overlapping in the middle between about 1770 and 1800.

Longcase clocks were made in two different forms, eight-day and thirty-hour. The thirty-hour was a cheaper clock and more often associated with country areas being made for cottage and farmhouse use. It follows that thirty-hour clocks were frequently smaller than eight-days of the same period, because of lower ceilings in cottages than in grander houses. When we examine dial sizes in relation to age; the smaller dial sizes will be found to persist longer in thirty-hour clocks than in eight-day clocks, because the case size was determined by the dial size, and cottage cases generally had to be kept small.

Arched dials were introduced as an alternative form to the square dial in about 1700, but were not widely popular till about 1720–30. The choice after about 1720 of a square or arched version lay with the customer as he could have either type. A clockmaker, by and large, made clocks to order and his customer would make the choice from the fashions which were currently available. In a city or large town a clockmaker might have a shop where he had some clocks completed and ready for sale. For most clockmakers, however, their 'shop' was their workshop and clocks were made to the customer's specifications within the parameters of styles the maker was familiar with. So the customer decided what he wanted, but the clockmaker was able to advise him on what styles were currently fashionable.

By about 1720 the arched dial was the newer and more fashionable type and it gained favour most strongly and most quickly in London, which of course was the centre of fashion. So when the arched dial took hold in London, it took an almost exclusive hold, which means that after about 1730 square dials were very much in the minority on London-made clocks. As the century progressed the arch-dial style became the normal London style, square examples being the exception thereafter.

London was the capital not only of the nation but also of clockmaking, and in the earlier years of longcase clockmaking led the field in style, which was copied to some considerable degree by provincial makers. Early provincial clocks, in dial style, followed the styles of London, but as the century progressed provincial makers increasingly went their own way. By mid century, many provincial clock dials are quite unlike London dials, and London rules of style cease to apply. In London itself the dial pattern was set by about 1730 and that pattern continued with very little change till the end of brass-dial clockmaking there.

In studying styles, then, we very soon have to learn to regard London as a distinctively separate style in dial-making terms after about 1730. The London influence spread into the home counties and to a lesser degree some larger cities, notably those where some makers wanted to copy the fashionable style of the capital. Edinburgh is a notable example, and Edinburgh dials often resemble London dials of about the same date. Some clockmakers moved their businesses from London out into provincial towns and cities, and so literally took the London style with them. Some provincial city makers would actually buy a dial from London, so they could offer the newest and most fashionable London style. More often, however, the local provincial town clockmaker would copy the London style he was readily familiar with.

Therefore, a London dial was always a readily identifiable style of its own after about 1730 and once seen it cannot be forgotten. But, of course, that London style will sometimes be found outside London, as just explained.

London dial sizes progressed from a ten-inch dial to eleven by about 1690, to twelve by about 1700 or a little later, and the interesting and distinctive thing is that it then stuck at twelve. Ten- and eleven-inch dials were almost always square. The arch came in at the twelve-inch mark and stayed. In the early years of the twelve-inch London dial some were square, but increasingly the arch was *the* style, and almost every London arch dial is a twelve-incher. Obviously these changes were gradual and one may have to give or take ten years in using them as a guide to age.

London was a nucleus of its own, not only in dial styles but in one other respect too, in that London longcase clocks were almost always eight-day examples (or longer running). The London trade catered for wealthy and sophisticated, perhaps fashion-conscious, customers from within the city and from all parts of the country too. They sought the custom of the upper income

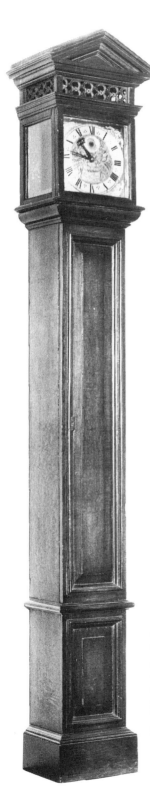

Exquisite nine-inch dial of thirty-hour quarter-chiming clock by John Williamson of London, dating from 1683. Striking hours and quarters on the same countwheel by means of a pump action system, using four bells. Plus points: rare strike/chime system, magnificently engraved floral decoration to centre.

Very slender 'coffin' type of case from the John Williamson clock and contemporary with the clock. Note the large side windows, typical of very early clocks. Also clock base is a continuation of the side members. Convex mould below hood and pitched pediment 'roof-top' hood are also features of this early period. Height about 7 ft. 8 in.

groups and offered a quality product of refined and tasteful style, and these customers were not the sort of people who were going to bother with daily winding. So London thirty-hour clocks do exist, but they are few and far between. This might be seen as making them 'scarce' or 'rare', but as we shall see later scarcity does not necessarily equate with high value. When we speak of any London longcase clock then, it goes without saying that we mean an eight-day, unless that term is qualified to specify anything other than an eight-day.

Early provincial dials copied London, but there was often a time lag of a few years in the spread of the London fashion. So a provincial dial might usually resemble in some degree the London style until about 1730, but a few years behind. By 1740 provincial dials were heading off along their own particular orbits, not out of ignorance of what London was doing, but by choice. Provincial dials, earlier ones in particular, show an amazing degree of local character and personality of the maker in them from this time on, whilst London dials became very repetitive to the point that when you've seen one London twelve-inch arched dial, you've seen nearly all of them.

It was not only in style that provincial makers soon went their own way, but also in size and shape. They began with ten-inch dials in eight-day clocks but a provincial ten-inch eight-day is very uncommon, simply because few makers were working in the provinces at this time. The same applies, though to a lesser degree, to eleven-inch provincial eight-day clocks. There were some counties where longcase clockmaking had barely begun by 1700, and in such counties the earliest eight-day clocks are likely to have twelve-inch dials, which by that time was the 'in' size. Unlike London, many provincial areas did not hold back dial size to twelve inches. Some areas such as the north-west of England, in particular, went on to dial sizes thirteen inches wide, some as early as the 1730s but more often by the 1770s. Size progressed to fourteen inches in some regions. In Lancashire, for instance, fourteen-inch brass dials were in use on grander eight-day clocks by the 1760s. Brass dials seldom exceeded fourteen inches anywhere at any time and the trend to the large size was mostly northern, especially north-western. Scotland was more restrained and there dial sizes were seldom larger than twelve inches and rarely exceeded thirteen.

Southern counties were more inclined to follow London trends, the more so the closer they were to London. In many southern counties dial sizes remained fixed at twelve inches.

At any period and anywhere it is possible to find a dial that does not conform to the regular pattern, so these guidelines can

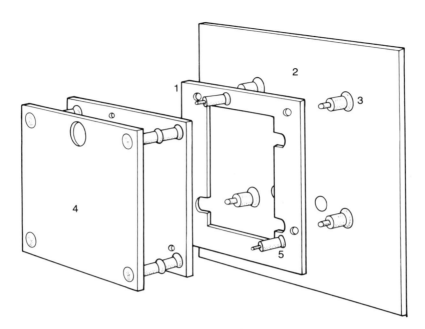

Principle of how a white dial is attached to the movement by means of a falseplate

1 Falseplate (iron)
2 Rear of white dial (iron, japanned on face, painted on rear)
3 Dial foot
4 Movement – this one is of plated form (brass)
5 Falseplate foot

never be taken as rigid. This nonconformity was more likely to happen in the north of England, where London had least influence anyway and where we have always been unruly. Nonconformity to regular size was also very likely in clocks with unusual features, such as those that played tunes, showed planetary conjunctions, etc., simply because these extras may have required a larger dial surface on which to be displayed.

Thirty-hour clocks in provincial areas where they were almost entirely confined, are a different story. The early ones have ten-inch dials, with just occasionally an early nine-inch or conceivably even eight. In the south dials tended to remain smaller than in the north, so here ten-inch thirty-hour clocks would date anywhere from 1690 to 1790 or even later. In some northern regions the ten-inch thirty-hour is unusual and here the starting size might more often have been eleven. Southern thirty-hours sometimes went to eleven inches in size, some later to twelve. In the north it was possible for even some very early makers to have started with the twelve-inch dial and thirteen-inch ones appeared later, but fourteen would be unusually large for any thirty-hour brass dial. As a very general rule, northern clockmakers seemed to prefer the bigger dials more often than their southern contemporaries.

As we have seen, the arch fashion appeared early in London and persisted. In the provinces one important factor was the overall case height, and clocks of the cottage type were made throughout almost the entire period of clockmaking. You could have either eight-day or thirty-hour clocks in the cottage style and so it was quite common for the square-dial fashion to linger on in provincial clocks even as late as the 1840s, as much as a hundred years later than square dials in London. At the same time grander eight-day clocks, presumably those made for customers with larger houses and taller ceilings, were often of the arched type. If a clock was to stand eight or nine feet high it would clearly have looked ridiculous with a tiny dial, and such clocks, especially in the north, would usually have the bigger dials, to keep the whole thing in some kind of proportion.

The question as to whether the clockmaker made his own brass dials or bought them from others is complicated and the answers are in many cases uncertain. A dial consisted of the actual dial sheet itself on to which were superimposed other separate pieces which were: the chapter ring (the circular band with numbering on), spandrels (the decorative cornerpieces) and sometimes other features such as a small chapter ring for the seconds dial and another for the calendar. The calendar was, however, more often displayed through a box-shaped aperture above the VI numeral with the numbers engraved on to a disc rotating behind the dial-sheet. Most clockmakers could make their own dial-sheets and other parts. What they could not all do was the engraving work of the numbers and dial centre design. They could also make the cast counterpieces, but for convenience would often buy these from a brass founder, and this is the reason that the number of patterns of spandrel found throughout the entire history of clockmaking is small – perhaps no more than thirty designs overall plus variations of those designs.

Those clockmakers who did their own engraving can sometimes be identified by the engraving quality and style. A beginner is unlikely to be able to recognize these from the alternative, which was the system whereby the clockmaker might make the chapter ring and send it away to a specialist engraver for the engraving work. Yet a third possibility was for the clockmaker to buy in a complete chapter ring already engraved with the numerals, which might have been easier than sending away his own ring for engraving, and not dramatically more

Nine-inch dial from a thirty-hour single-handed clock by John Waklin. Plus points: small size, early period (*circa* 1710), extremely fine engraving, original hand of unusual style. The movement is of the posted type.

expensive. He might possibly buy in several chapter rings at once rather than attempt to order them one by one, and this was often the case if he were in a more remote area or some long distance from his nearest supplier.

Buying in chapter rings in batches might explain the occasional inconsistency sometimes met with whereby the wrong kind of chapter ring has been used. For example, I once bought a thirty-hour two-handed clock with a one-handed chapter ring, which is something which would almost always be a case of a later alteration but, in this particular instance, and I only ever came across the one example, it was made that way originally. One can imagine the situation where an order for a clock was called for urgently and the only chapter rings left in stock were one-handers. New supplies might have taken weeks to be delivered, so the clockmaker 'made do' with what he had on hand. Clockmakers would sometimes make last minute modifications to a clock as an expediency, and these can be puzzling as it is often difficult to identify when an alteration is part of the original work and when it has been done much later. The latter is by far the most common explanation and later alteration of any kind will usually switch off any serious buyer.

How can you tell whether the clockmaker did his own engraving or bought in his engraved work, and does it really matter? Well mostly it does not matter. One should assess a clock's merits by its quality, rather than on a who-did-what basis. Clearly it is 'better' if the clock has good engraving throughout. If we think of an extreme example it may put this into perspective: let's say a clock made by a very famous maker such as Thomas Tompion or Joseph Knibb. These people were making clocks for wealthy customers and hopefully were offering the best clock money could buy of its kind. Are we to imagine that these men sat down at a bench engraving chapter rings? Not for one moment. Tompion employed journeyman clockmakers to do all that for him, separate and anonymous craftsmen who worked 'in house'. Therefore, if you buy a Tompion clock you are buying an item which may have been made by several unknown journeymen and which was sold under the Tompion label, and it is none the worse for that. So in the search for 'quality' of product, one assesses the whole regardless of whether the maker made the whole of it or none of it (as in Tompion's case). Tompion was in a sense a workmaster, designer and chief quality controller!

On the other hand if you *can* identify the fact that the maker did make it all himself, then there is more satisfaction and interest in knowing that. One clockmaker who worked not two miles from where I live was Will Snow of Padside in North Yorkshire and I've handled a good many clocks of his over the years. He did things in his own unique and somewhat eccentric manner and from experience I can now recognize aspects of his clocks that demonstrate to me that he did actually make them himself. A novice cannot hope to begin to recognize such things as he may never have seen another example of a clock by a maker whose work he is studying and, if he did, he probably cannot remember vital details of comparison.

What a beginner often *can* recognize is the example where the dial sheet engraving is different in style and usually of much lower quality of execution than the chapter ring engraving. This will apply almost exclusively to provincial makers and principally to those in country areas. There may be some satisfaction in knowing that the clockmaker did actually perform the constructional work himself, even if he was not an engraver and had to buy in his chapter ring work. In terms of character, individuality, craftsmanship and sheer interest, the product of a craftsman who *can* be seen to have done his own engraving is clearly the optimum.

Such a clock will have a personality of its own, though it may be an 'inferior' item in artistic style and skill to a more stereotyped product such as a later eighteenth-century London clock, which may be no more than a clone of its neighbour. So the personality and individuality of the one-man-band clockmaker's product does not necessarily equate with quality, biggest demand or highest price. The best work of a provincial maker might be full of character and interest and the mark of his own handiwork, but inferior in quality of style or execution, or both, compared to a mediocre London clock displaying none of those things. Commercial demand as reflected in high prices today is not necessarily a reflection of the effort or dedication a clockmaker put into his work, nor of his own personal skills. Much of it, unfortunately, is based on present-day whims and fancies.

A different kind of brass dial appeared by the late 1760s, but more commonly was found towards the end of the eighteenth century. This consisted of a single sheet of brass with the numbers and the decorative features, if any, engraved directly on to the one sheet of brass. In other words, these had no separate chapter ring or spandrels. This is known today as the one-piece dial or the single-sheet dial – what they called it at the time we do not know. For the most part this type of dial was the brass-dial maker's answer to the painted dial. The one-piece dial was silvered over its entire surface when new, and might sometimes be called a silver or silvered dial.

This surface is not solid silver, but a coating which is applied as a finishing touch. The silvering was done by an application of silver chloride paste, which was sealed with a coating of lacquer over the surface. Without the sealing of the lacquer the dial would soon blacken from contact with the atmosphere. The earlier kind of composite brass dial was also silvered, generally over its engraved areas – namely chapter ring(s), calendar ring, nameplate and the dial centre (but only when the dial centre was a polished type with an engraved pattern). A matted centre could not be silvered. Silvering was often worn away by owners who polished regularly, and many clocks today show no signs of silvering because it has all been polished away. Restorers usually re-silver a dial, which in any event will have been re-silvered many times during its life, as silvering will seldom last beyond twenty years or so.

The single-sheet dial was a style mainly of the 1780s and 1790s, and ran until perhaps 1810 at the latest. Exceptionally it was used later still, notably in round-dial clocks, but also in arched and sometimes square form, in London and in the West Country where examples from as late as the 1840s are found. Such late West Country clocks are often mistakenly dated too early because of this dial style.

Dial size, when used in conjunction with the type of clock (eight-day London, thirty-hour northern provincial, etc) can be a helpful indicator of age, even if one knows nothing at all about dial styles. The dial style, on the other hand, is a much more accurate guide towards age and will enable the experienced to date a clock within five years either way. For this reason clock enthusiasts don't refer to clocks by such vague terms as Georgian, which after all covers the period from 1714 to 1830 and would therefore cover the majority of clocks met with. Auctioneers sometimes use this term, but clock collectors don't because they can assess the age more accurately.

It is perfectly obvious that a ten-inch square eight-day London dial of about 1690 will look very different from a thirteen-inch 1790 dial from Lancashire. The sheer size difference alone will enforce differences of proportion, especially in the chapter ring width and therefore the size of the numbers. The chapter ring of the former might be as narrow as one inch, whilst the latter two and a half or even three inches wide. So we are looking not only at size, but also relative proportion. An early dial will have very small minute numbers marked 5,10,15 and relatively large hour numbers marked I,II,III. The minute numbers begin *inside* the minute band, progress to outside by about 1690, and grow progressively larger from then onwards. An early example might have the hour numbers proportionate in size to the minute numbers in a ratio of five to one, a late example more like two to

Eleven-inch thirty-hour clock of about 1760 by John Stancliffe of Barkisland, near Halifax. The moon dial of penny type and chapter-ring engraving are plus factors. Negative factor: poor dial centre engraving.

one. So as far as the numerals are concerned the minute figures grow progressively over the years in relation to the hours. A London dial, which as we have seen, remained at the twelve-inch width, might progress to a ratio of two to one, although the numbers would be much smaller than on a fourteen-inch Lancashire dial just because of sheer size difference of the chapter ring.

On the inside rim of the chapter ring early two-handed clocks mark units of four to the hour (quarter hours), the half-hour point usually being indicated by a large fleur-de-lys or other decorative symbol. By about 1760 the quarter-hour and half-hour indications cease to appear, leaving only engraved hours and minutes. Therefore a chapter ring of 1780 looks very different from one of say 1730, not only because of its very different proportions but also as a result of the engraved work on it. There is a reason for these inner quarter-hour markers, but to understand it we must first look at a single-handed clock dial.

Lantern clocks had a single hand and indicated hours and quarters only; minutes were not marked. A very small number of lantern clocks did mark minutes and have two hands, but you are unlikely to come across a genuine one. Early single-handed longcase clocks were in a sense cased versions of a lantern clock, though the movements could be posted (like a lantern clock) or plate framed (like an eight-day longcase). The option to have your longcase clock with one hand or two was open to the customer. Eight-day clocks were virtually always two-handers, thirty-hour clocks more frequently adopted the two-handed form as time went by. Therefore, by 1760 single-handers were virtually obsolete except in a few traditional areas such as East Anglia where the old single-handed option was still available on request.

A single-handed clock was legible and made sense to all. After all, a sundial only casts a single shadow and they had been familiar objects for generations. In the late seventeenth century and early eighteenth a clock might appear in a house for the first time as that buyer might be the first person in the history of his family to have purchased a clock of any kind. A single hand could be understood by all – even those people who had never had a clock before. Two hands must have been very confusing to such first-time owners. This is one reason the hands on a two-hander were made so very different to each other in these earlier times.

Many early eight-day clocks, indeed all the earliest ones until perhaps 1730 and later still in provincial areas, marked the inner chapter ring with what were in effect the same markings as on a single-handed clock. This meant that anyone unfamiliar with the 'new-fangled' two-handed business of minutes and hours could,

Single-sheet thirteen-inch brass-dial clock by James Peddie of Stirling of about 1790. The engraving is typical of many clocks of this type. Plus factors: good engraving work, original hands. Negative points: single-sheet dial.

if he wished, read the clock in exactly the same way as a single-hander by ignoring the minute hand and reading the time from the hour hand.

Before the time of two-handed clocks, that is before the introduction of the pendulum in 1658, the customary unit of time was the quarter hour or, if you wanted to be more precise, the half-quarter (of an hour). Early two-handed clocks often mark the half-quarter unit by means of an asterisk or other symbol on the chapter ring between the 5- and 10-minute numbers at 7½ minutes past. This was read from the minute hand, which already pointed to quarter hours, and so only the *half* quarters were designated, namely at 7½ minutes and 22½ minutes past, and to, the hour. Half-quarter markings dropped from use by about 1730.

Corner spandrels went through a series of patterns, each one lasting roughly a generation (twenty years), and there were usually several patterns available at any one time. These patterns are illustrated as comprehensibly as possible in my own book, *Grandfather Clocks and their Cases*. Knowledge of spandrel styles can in itself be a good guide to dating a clock, assuming that the dial has the original spandrels. To check their originality, look for any spare holes in the dial-plate (best seen from the back) where previous ones might have fitted.

Early seconds dials are usually marked 5,10,15 etc. Later ones normally run 10,20,30, but this is not an infallible sequence.

So far we have discussed only brass dials. Painted dials came in a year or two before 1775 and within ten years were known throughout the land and within twenty years had virtually replaced the brass dial everywhere, with the possible exception of London which was set in its brass-dial ways. White dials, as they were then called and sometimes still are, were manufactured by specialist dial-making concerns, the majority of which were in Birmingham. The process was that known as 'japanning' whereby an iron sheet was coated in a kind of paint that was furnace-hardened and then handpainted with flowers or other designs according to the fashion of the day.

The first advertisement, that we know of, for the new kind of dials was placed in 1772 by Messrs Osborne & Wilson of Birmingham who were partners until 1777, after which time each traded separately. James Wilson died in 1809; Thomas Osborne died in 1779, but his widow and son carried on the business till about 1813. Most white dials of the eighteenth century carry the imprint of Osborne or Wilson or of the partnership period, though Wilson dials considerably outnumber those by Osborne which suggest he was more successful commercially.

Many white dials, particularly the earlier ones, were supplied

Representative corner spandrel from a longcase dial.
The centre cherub head theme occurs on many
spandrels in a variety of forms.

with an iron backing-plate, called a falseplate, by means of which
each could be attached to its movement. Very often the falseplate
was impressed with the name of the dial-maker and as the names
of dial-makers are well documented this provides a very useful
secondary means of identification, authentication and dating. To
check on the full story of this kind of dial and full lists of all
known dial-making concerns you may like to consult my book
White Dial Clocks: The Complete Guide.

Most white dials were made in Birmingham, and this place
name is imprinted on many falseplates along with that of the
dial-maker. This gave rise in the past to the misconception that
such clocks were completely 'made in Birmingham' and until
recent times they were much misunderstood and undervalued. In
fact the local clockmaker continued to make his own movements
just as he had with brass dials, and the presence of a falseplate
behind such a dial can be an indication of the fact that the clock
was made by a local maker. By the time clocks were standardized
to the point where they could be bought in complete with dial by
a retailer, there was in fact no need to use the falseplate at all.
After about 1830 when this was the case, falseplates appeared less
often. Thirty-hour clocks hardly ever had falseplates at any time
(but sometimes for a particular reason an eight-day dial and
falseplate were used for a thirty-hour clock). Brass-dial clocks did
not have falseplates at all, and those that do today have been
made up from parts of other clocks – this aspect is discussed
further in Chapter 8.

White dials were also made in other places besides
Birmingham, such as Halifax and Newcastle on Tyne. The first
Scottish ones were made in Edinburgh towards the end of the
eighteenth century, prior to which Scottish white-dial clocks have
English-made dials which can be established by the dial-maker's

name impressed behind the dial or on the falseplate. With experience it is possible to recognize an English dial from a Scottish one by its style. The novice obviously lacks this experience and will have to rely on the falseplate imprint or that behind the dial for identification. This is often on the back of the calendar-wheel or moon-wheel and can be difficult to spot on a clock which is fully assembled. It is not difficult to learn the technique of peering into the clock from the side of the movement with the aid of a torch in such a way that the impressed mark can be read.

Whether the dial was made in England or Scotland is much less important than whether or not it is attractive and of good quality. The quality of painted dials decreased as time went on and by the 1850s they were cheaper in quality and price than they had been seventy years before. They were also less restrained in artistic terms and even gaudy or poorly painted. A very late English dial can be a poor thing at the best of times. A late Scottish one, however, can be even worse. As a novice you may be unable to locate the dial-maker's imprint (many Scottish dials and some English dials don't have one), and you will have to judge the age of the dial by its style which is a very simple process once you get the hang of it.

The styles of painted dials fall very conveniently into three phases, each easily recognizable once you know the basics. The first period ran from the beginning (1772) to 1800, during which time the dials had a largely plain white, or slightly off-white background, with a little colour in the corners and also on the top of the arched dial. The corner decoration was usually a spray of flowers or a single flower, such as a rose or carnation, or even a cluster of strawberries. The corner painting would be surrounded by a raised border of dot-dash patterned gold paint. For convenience I call these dials 'strawberry corner' style, whether actually strawberries or flowers, for want of a better term to describe them. Colours are usually delicate with gentle pinks predominating. On some of these first-period dials the corner work is a gold-painted scroll pattern, resembling vaguely in paintwork a brass-dial spandrel pattern. The arch might have a central feature such as a name panel, a central flower spray or a bird perhaps, at each side of which would be another decorative section similar to the dial corners. Towards the end of the century the arch would often have a central oval painted panel showing a pastoral scene such as a shepherdess. Right at the end of the century the arch scene might be a solid landscape showing a shooting scene, a landscape or such like.

The most easily distinctive feature of a period one dial is the

Thirteen-inch dial of eight-day rolling moon longcase clock by John Callcott of Cotton in Shropshire, actually dated 1819. Plus features: moon dial and known date.

numbering pattern. Minutes were marked by dots, every fifth one being numbered: 5,10,15, etc. in Arabic numbers. The hours were marked underneath these in Roman numerals I,II,III,IIII, etc. The presence of a seconds dial, calendar dial, name of maker, or perhaps a moon dial does not affect this overall style and numbering pattern. Exactly the same numbering pattern was used on brass dials of this same period.

At the beginning of the second period, 1800–30, corner designs were more often composed of geometric patterns such as fans, ovals and concentric rings of colours which are sometimes centred by a shell motif. Painted decoration at this time may vary a lot, often with more colour over a larger area (though still within the corner sections) and often with bolder colours (strong reds, greens or blues). About 1800 (give or take five years) the numbering pattern changed in two ways. The hours were now marked with large Arabic numbers, 1,2,3,4, etc., which were sometimes positioned vertically but were more often what is known as 'tumbling numbers', which means 1,2,3 were placed radially to the centre, 4 to 8 inverted and 9 to 12 re-inverted to keep the numbers more or less upright from the observer's point of view. For a brief time the Arabic hours ran together with Arabic 5-, 10- and 15-minute marking. (A few late dials by Wilson are of this pattern.) With the beginning of the nineteenth century, however, the minutes increasingly ceased to be marked at the 5- and 10- minute divisions and only quarter-hour minutes were shown thereafter (60,15,30,45). The actual minutes were no longer marked by dots but by an enclosed double circle of markings. An asterisk was sometimes positioned where the 5, 10,20,25,35,40,50 and 55 numbers had previously been. Arabic hour numbers never really settled down as they didn't quite suit a clock dial.

Period three started about 1830 and at this time the hour numbers returned to the previous Roman form (I,II,III,IIII, etc) with minutes ceasing to be numbered at all. This meant that the hour numbers were larger as they occupied the space formerly taken up by minutes and hours together. Therefore period three Roman hour numbers are much bolder than those in period one. The painted decoration in the corners and arch were bolder too in this period with each corner usually being entirely filled by a painted landscape scene, with another solid painting in the arch. Sometimes themes which split conveniently into four were used: the four seasons, four continents, etc. Painting was now bolder, heavier, often crude and even gaudy. Sometimes silver leaf was used underneath the paint to give the colours a vivid iridescent glow especially effective with blues, greens and reds on some Scottish dials. Some later period three dials are primitive, akin to

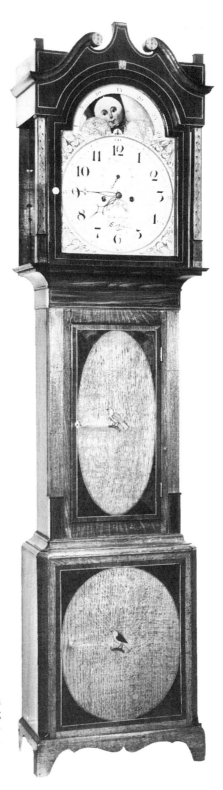

Case of the John Callcott clock, oak with
unusual amount of mahogany trim, standing
only 7 ft. 2 in. Plus factors: clean condition,
unusual bird marquetry inlays.

fairground painting or canal boat painting. Landscapes passed reasonably well, but figures usually let these paintings down badly.

An indication of the lowering of quality which took place between the 1770s and the 1860s, and which arose from the struggle of competition between increasing numbers of dial-makers, can be seen in the prices. If we took an example of an eight-day solid arch thirteen-inch dial as an example, the price in the 1770s was around one pound and in the 1860s 7s 6d (75p). Not only were the dials of the Wilson period generally more attractive, but the quality of japanning was better and these dials are often better preserved despite their greater age. A pound at that time represented a good week's wages to a skilled craftsman.

The earliest clock hands were made of steel and they were cut, cleaned up by filing, chamfered and bevelled. Before fitting the hands were 'blued', that is heated in iron filings till they turned a blue-black colour. The colour was stabilized by rubbing with oil or lacquering. The patterns of the early hands were what we call non-matching, in that the hour and minute hands were distinctly different from each other; the point being that they could not be confused with one another. On a single-handed clock the one (hour) hand would have a projecting 'tail' used for leverage when resetting the time.

By the 1790s matching hands began to appear, being of such a style that the minute hand was a longer and slimmer version of the hour hand. These were initially still made of steel, though brass hands first appeared as matching pairs in the late eighteenth century. Very occasionally particular makers used brass for making non-matching hands before about 1790. By the beginning of the nineteenth century the fashion for matching hands was increasingly to make them in brass, and matching steel hands dropped from use by about 1820 to 1830 in longcases. In bracket clocks and wall clocks they lingered slightly later as brass was less often used for the hands of wall clocks or bracket clocks.

Early matching hands were simple, with diamond-shaped or crescent-shaped tips. Later ones, especially in brass, became very ornate and might incorporate crowns, acorns or multi-pierced designs; the brass surface was often decorated with punch-patterns. These later and more ornate hands may look superficially more splendid, but were less difficult to make than the earlier steel hands. Hand patterns must be studied to be learned. The original hands may be an important factor in a clock's appeal. If broken or missing hands are to be replaced, it is important that the correct style is used or the whole appearance of the clock can be spoiled.

How do you assess quality in a brass dial? What makes one superb and one miserable? Does it matter anyway and are other things such as age more important than quality? Well there is a quality factor which is easily seen even by a beginner. If you could examine half a dozen dials of varying quality for ten minutes, you would know for evermore all about dial quality. You can, however, try doing that by means of the illustrations in this book.

Quality was often a sign of that extra effort and pride one clockmaker took in his work over and above what another, less able or less caring clockmaker did. Generally speaking, age has a bearing on quality. Clockmakers of say 1700 might well take a greater pride in the appearance of their work than those of 1800. Quality decreased as time went by, sometimes in an effort to cut corners and keep prices low enough to compete with others. There always were, and still are, customers who care more about a cheap price than a quality product. A poor quality clock will often keep time just as good as a better one, last equally long and behave as reliably. Any clock which still runs after 200 years can hardly have been a poor thing, but it could well be of low quality alongside its peers. Clockmakers would often produce two grades of work. Thomas Lister (junior) of Halifax made some magnificent and highly complicated clocks, works of genius in fact. But his average thirty-hour clock can at times be a very ordinary product.

By 1700 the London brass dial style was established and other London clockmakers following on were producing a style which changed only slowly. There the measure of quality was not in the style, but in the quality of execution of that style. A matted centre with ringed winding holes, square box calendar and maybe a little engraving in the matted ground around the datebox was usually done to a set high standard. In the provinces, however, a clockmaker was more able to express his individualities of style. If he copied the London style and was measured against that, he might fail to quite come up to the London level. But if he gave free range to his own individual stylistic inclinations, he might produce a dial full of personality and character and of first-class workmanship, and it would be wrong to measure this kind of style by its resemblance or otherwise to contemporary London work. So all-over engraving on a polished dial centre (as opposed to a London matted centre) is a very different stylistic treatment and can only be compared with examples of its own kind of style.

It is easy to measure the skill of an engraver's dial centre design. Is it balanced, carefully and boldly done, lacking in artistry design wise or feebly engraved with a lack of confidence? It does not take long to distinguish good from bad. But the fact

solid line = normal
dotted line = unusual

BRASS DIALS   EITHER   WHITE DIAL

1680 1690 1700 1710 1720 1730 1740 1750 1760 1770 1780 1790 1800 1810 1820 1830 1840 1850 1860

DIAL FEATURES
square dials
arched dials
round dials
dotted minutes
double minute band
roman hours I,II,III
arabic hours 1,2,3
minutes numbered 5,10,15
minutes numbered 15,30,45,60
minutes not numbered
half-hour markers
inner quarters marked
half quarters marked
tidal dials
rocking figure

DIAL SIZES
10 inch 8 day
10 inch 30 hour
11 inch 8 day
11 inch 30 hour
12 inch 8 day
12 inch 30 hour
13 inch 8 day
13 inch 30 hour
14 inch 8 day
14 inch 30 hour
15 inch 8 day or 30 hour

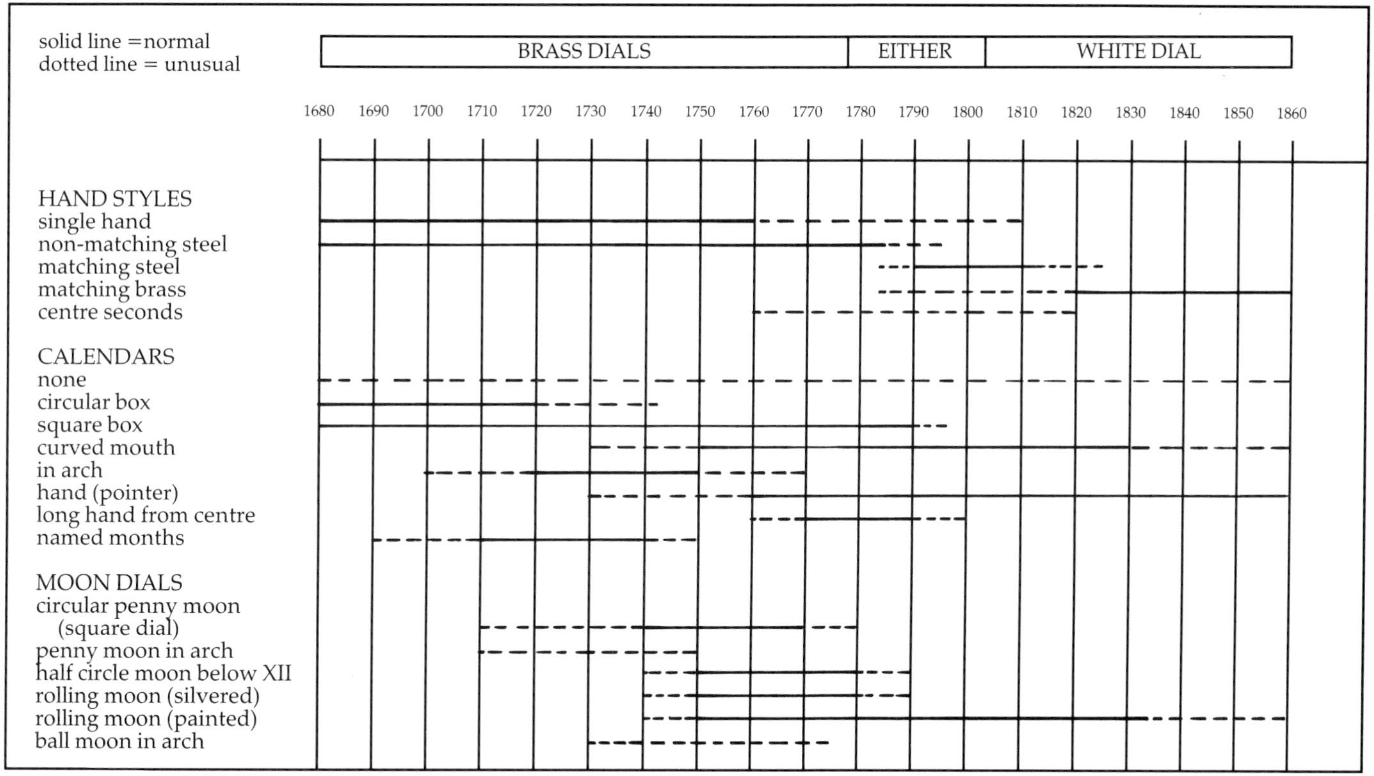

solid line =normal
dotted line = unusual
BRASS DIALS
EITHER
WHITE DIAL
1680
1690
1700
1710
1720
1730
1740
1750
1760
1770
1780
1790
1800
1810
1820
1830
1840
1850
1860
HAND STYLES
single hand
non-matching steel
matching steel
matching brass
centre seconds
CALENDARS
none
circular box
square box
curved mouth
in arch
hand (pointer)
long hand from centre
named months
MOON DIALS
circular penny moon
(square dial)
penny moon in arch
half circle moon below XII
rolling moon (silvered)
rolling moon (painted)
ball moon in arch

that there was perhaps very little dial centre engraving on a London clock was not because that maker was incapable of doing it, but because the London fashion of the day did not call for it. You have only to look at a few clock dials to be able to see which are the better ones, or, what is perhaps more important for you as a potential buyer, the ones which you personally like best. If you don't read a book or two and compare a few dials, you have no idea of the range that exists, and you may well be seduced by the first dial you come across, only to find later, when you do compare it with others, that it is a bit of a mundane thing. Most people only intend to buy one clock, so you might as well take the opportunity of learning how to differentiate between various types. Most people who now own a small collection of clocks only ever set out initially to buy a single example, and you could very soon join them, so don't dash out and buy the first thing you bump into – learn to distinguish.

DATING CHARTS

The two charts on pages 44 and 45 attempt to summarize stylistic trends in diagrammatic form so that the information is available at a glance. In other words they attempt the impossible. Reading off the required features on these charts will offer an accurate result for many clocks most of the time. They will not work for all clocks all of the time.

The charts must therefore be used cautiously. For instance, they assume that brass-dial clocks were entirely replaced by white-dials by the year 1800. In reality no such definite cut-off point exists. Brass dials of the single-sheet type continued in use on some regulators, some round-dial longcases (particularly in Scotland), some London longcases, and some late longcases in the West Country (Devon, Somerset, etc). For most clocks, however, longcases especially, any brass dial will usually date from before 1800. Naturally, in reproduction clocks such as those longcases of 1890 imitating those of 1790, the charts will not hold true. Nor will they for fakes or altered clocks. So use the charts with common sense and they should prove to be very useful.

The charts are drawn up principally with longcase clocks in mind for which they will work best. They will work to a lesser degree for bracket clocks, but with some of the more esoteric types of clock, such as tavern clocks, they will be less reliable.

2 What Goes on Inside a Clock

Clocks have their own vocabulary of a dozen or so specialized words. If you don't understand them at first it does not matter as you will find you soon pick up the habit of using them.

The works of a clock are known as the movement. Inside the movement are the gears, referred to as wheels, which are made of brass. They are linked by smaller wheels of steel, known as pinions. The theory is that different metals in constant contact wear less than like metals doing the same. Therefore in most clocks, brass wheels engage with steel pinions. Novices are frequently amazed to see that a set of wheels and pinions can still work after 200 or even 300 years and show surprisingly little wear, all things considered. The reason is partly because of this use of different metals. Oddly enough it is usually the harder steel that shows signs of wear before the softer brass. One reason for this is that steel rusts and brass does not. Another factor is that in operation the brass wheels get tiny grains of steel embedded into them which then grind into the steel pinions. Often, of course, a clock may have been standing unused for some considerable part of its life, as there were periods when they fell out of fashion.

The wheels and pinions in a longcase clock are quite large. If damage or wear occurs, it is usually possible to mend a wheel rather than replace it. If a wheel suffers breakage of one or more teeth, then the practice is to replace the teeth, not the wheel, which enables many a repaired wheel to run happily years later. In any case, clock wheels are not interchangeable, so it is not possible simply to take a spare out of some scrap clock and use that. A new wheel has to be measured and cut accurately to the dimensions of the old. This is a nuisance and costly enough to have made restorers inclined to mend rather than replace. So, as a result, sheer economics have assisted conservation.

A set of wheels is known as a train. One train drives the clock itself and this is known as the going train. The train which drives the strikework is called the strike train. Sometimes a third might drive a chime or musical feature. Each train in a clock requires its own power supply which might be a weight or a spring.

A weight provides a more consistent power source as it pulls equally strongly whether fully wound or almost run down. A spring pulls strongly when fully wound and weakly when almost run down. Weights were therefore favoured for driving the great majority of British clocks – principally lantern clocks and certain types of wall clocks (tavern clocks and hooded clocks) as well as longcase clocks. Weights had other advantages too in offering a more robust system than a spring. Any spring will sooner or later fail from metal fatigue. Furthermore with a weight-driven clock there was no danger of over-winding.

Spring-making was a difficult art involving hammering a piece of steel till it was several feet long, then coiling it up into a roll so that it could be tensioned and released repeatedly without breaking. British spring clocks contained an extra gear known as a fusee, a cone-shaped device carrying the driving line and positioned so that when the spring was fully wound it had to pull against the smaller, more resistant end, and when nearly run down it had to pull against the wider, less resistant end. The fusee gear was an attempt to average out the varying strength of a spring, so it never appears in a weight clock. It worked to some degree, but never to the degree of the unvarying consistency of a weight. For these reasons spring clocks were more difficult to make than weight clocks and were more costly. Any clockmaker could make weight clocks, but this was not so with spring clocks which tended to be concentrated amongst more specialized makers. Strangely enough the word fusee (pronounced fyuzee) is of French origin, yet French clocks seldom have them. In the past the word was sometimes pronounced 'fuzzy' by English clockmakers. However you pronounce it today any clock enthusiast will know what you mean.

Every clock has an escapement which is an interrupter device to slow down the speed at which the clock wheels turn. It is the sound of the escapement one hears when a clock ticks. If there was no escapement the clock wheels would spin rapidly round as soon as the power source was wound up and the clock would run down instantly as the weight crashed to the ground. The escapement regulates the clock speed to a measurable pace and that pace is determined by the length of the pendulum. On a longcase clock that pace is usually a one-second unit, so most longcase clocks tick once a second. They don't have to tick at that pace, however, and all kinds of variations are possible, though unusual.

Most longcase clocks have an anchor escapement – in fact almost all do. This is sometimes known as a recoil escapement. When the clock ticks, the second hand (attached to the

The Anchor Escapement

1 Anchor   3 Pallet faces
2 Pallet   4 Escape wheel

The Deadbeat Escapement

1 Anchor   3 Pallet faces
2 Pallet   4 Escape wheel

escape-wheel arbor) can be seen to recoil slightly at each beat. A modified form of anchor escapement is called a deadbeat escapement which is still a type of anchor, but more accurately formed in such a way that there is no recoil. A seconds hand on a deadbeat clock would therefore stop dead at each beat.

The verge escapement pre-dates the anchor, but was entirely replaced by the anchor in longcase clocks by about 1680. In bracket clocks the verge escapement was used till about 1790 when the anchor finally replaced it. In lantern clocks the verge was used increasingly less often than the anchor till lantern clocks died out in the 1790s. You are unlikely to see a longcase clock with verge escapement today.

Wheels and pinions turn on axles known as arbors. An arbor was thinned down at each end where its bearing surface meets the clock plates and these points are called pivots. Wear often takes place at the points in the plates where the pivots turn, so pivot holes may become elongated thus altering the intended position of the wheels and their contact. Worn pivot holes can be bushed whereby a brass plug is inserted with a truly-drilled pivot hole, thus putting wheels back into true alignment.

Two basic kinds of longcase movement exist: the eight-day and the thirty-hour. A thirty-hour clock has a continuous rope or chain and a single weight, which produces both striking and going power. Eight-day clocks have two weights: one each for the going and striking trains. An eight-day clock without strikework would obviously only have a single train and a single weight and such a clock is called a timepiece. The word 'timepiece' is sometimes used incorrectly as an alternative for the word 'clock', but strictly-speaking a timepiece is a non-striking clock.

Clocks exist which run longer than eight days. Some run for a month, three months, six months or even a year, just on one winding. An eight-day has a going train of four wheels, a month clock or a three-month clock has five and a six-month or a year clock has six. Eight-day and longer duration clocks wind with a crank key through holes in the dial. An eight-day clock winds clockwise (almost always), a month or three-month clock anti-clockwise and a six-month or a year clock clockwise. Month clocks are uncommon. Anything running longer than a month is a very rare item.

A lantern clock was always of thirty-hour duration, less in some early examples. The clock was known as a posted-frame construction, whereby four upright corner posts support a top and bottom plate. The wheels are held between upright bars within this 'cage'. Some thirty-hour longcase clocks are also constructed on the same principle. This type of movement has

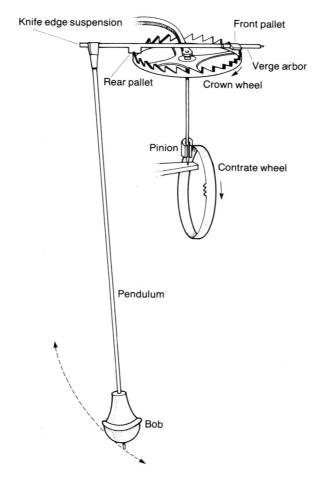

Knife edge suspension

Front pallet

Verge arbor

Rear pallet

Crown wheel

Pinion

Contrate wheel

Pendulum

Bob

Principle of the verge pendulum or bob pendulum

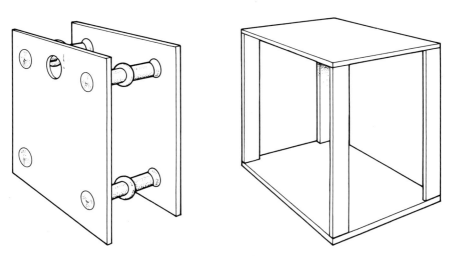

Movement layout systems showing plate-frame construction (*left*) and posted construction (*right*), sometimes known as a birdcage.

several alternative names. It could be called any of the following: a lantern movement, post-framed movement, posted movement or sometimes a birdcage movement. The birdcage movement was used in earlier periods in many areas (before about 1720), but in the south it was used for much longer (till approximately 1790) by those makers who opted for this form. Those who didn't used the plated construction which is along the same principle as an eight-day. Occasionally, posted-movement longcases occur as late as the 1820s (for example in East Anglia).

A thirty-hour clock could at any period have been made with a plate-framed movement, like an eight-day. This has a vertical plate front and back, held apart by four pillars. The wheels are pivoted between the two plates. By the late eighteenth century almost all thirty-hour clocks used this plated form (considerably earlier in the north), which was the same form as that used for eight-day or longer duration clocks.

Eight-day clocks were never of birdcage construction. Because it was a fashion almost exclusive to the south, the birdcage movement is met with less frequently than the plated form. It is not in itself a 'scarcer' or better form, but more often an indication of a regional trend. The birdcage was unusual in northern clocks and there its use is almost always a sign of greater age and therefore scarcity.

Birdcage movements had four corner posts of brass or iron which were either round or square. The shape and metal were largely a whim of the individual maker. Plated movements usually had pillars of brass, but just occasionally they were made of iron. Plated movements mostly have four pillars – birdcage movements always have four. London-plated clocks, and those influenced by London, very often have five pillars. Occasionally, early London clocks have six or even more pillars, but this is most likely to be on clocks of long duration or on those which might need to be stronger than normal. The number of pillars is not necessarily a sign of higher quality, though it can be. More than five pillars is usually a sign of greater age.

Some clocks, principally early London clocks before about 1700, have latches which are sometimes referred to as latched pillars. The latches were on the front plate and were used to lock the plates together after assembly instead of the usual pinned method. Some clocks, usually those by earlier London makers of repute, also had latched dial feet which meant that the dial clipped in place rather than pinning in the normal manner. Latched pillars and latched dial feet are both thought of as signs of high quality work and seldom occur after about 1720.

All British longcase clocks strike the hour (except timepieces).

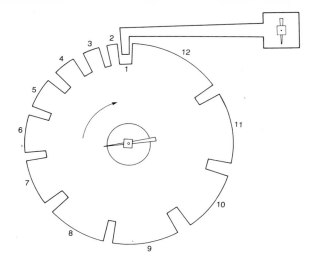

Countwheel striking system, also known as locking-plate striking. During striking the arm (detent) is held out of the notch in the countwheel, an ever-increasing space for each hour returning to 1 again after 12.

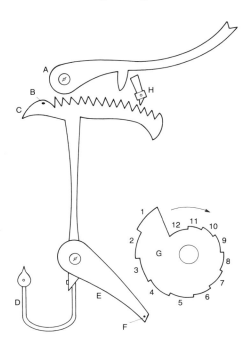

The principle of rack striking. The spring (D) pushes the rack (C) left so that the gathering pallet (H) can pick up the required number of teeth. A pin (F) on the rack tail (E) comes to rest against the stepped edge of the snail (G) offering the required count. The rack hook is (A). This system allows for the last hour to be repeated at will by means of a repeater trigger.

British clocks do not normally strike half hours, though some have been modified to strike a single blow at half-past in the way that many French clocks do. Quarter-hour chiming is a special function, usually driven through a third train. On longcases made before 1870 it is quite rare, but is less so on bracket clocks. Many German-made clocks (though made for the British market) dating from the end of the nineteenth century do chime quarter hours and these are very commonplace.

Striking was initially controlled by a countwheel or locking plate, being two different terms used to describe the same thing, namely a wheel with notches spaced at increasing intervals round its rim. The clock struck as long as a lever was held out of the notch, until the next notch came round. Count-wheel striking was used on thirty-hour clocks throughout their entire period of manufacture. Exceptionally a thirty-hour was made with rack striking so that it could be used as a repeater. Count-wheel striking on eight-day clocks was used from the beginning until replaced by rack striking, which was supposedly invented in the 1670s, but took some considerable time to come into widespread use. On early eight-day clocks count wheels were placed outside the movement at the back and these were known as outside countwheels. Later it was replaced inside the movement (after about 1490), and this is known as inside countwheel striking. Thirty-hours always had count wheels outside.

By the 1690s many eight-day London clocks had rack striking, though count wheel striking remained a while longer. In other areas, especially north-west England, rack striking was slow to come into use, perhaps because it had certain disadvantages. It involved the use of a spring, which sooner or later would fail. On many rack striking clocks also, it was often possible to damage the strikework or jam the clock, or both, if the hands were wound through twelve without striking, or if the strike train inadvertently ran down before the going train (thus also forcing the hands through twelve without striking). So some provincial makers retained the countwheel system which had none of these faults for long after rack striking was known. Some Lancashire eight-day clocks, for instance, still retain count-wheel striking as late as 1800; a thing which is unheard-of in the south.

The presence of count-wheel striking, therefore, is normal on thirty-hour clocks. It can be an indication of age on eight-day clocks, but should not automatically be taken as such and may often be more of a regional preference than a period indicator.

Rack striking was often referred to as rack repeating in its early days. This is because its presence enabled the clock to be repeated by pulling a cord, which meant it could re-strike the past hour. It

Twelve-inch dial of the eight-day clock by John Waklin. Plus points: herringbone edge engraving, superb centre engraving, bold design, original hands (despite eccentric patterns). Very early clocks such as this often have the signature below the chapter ring on the main dial plate, as here.

Eight-day clock by John Waklin in ebonized pine case standing 6 ft. 10 in from about 1700–10. Plus points: age, proportion and restrained height. Negative points: black cases are not as popular as 'coloured' woods.

-Movement of the John Waklin clock with unusual features indicative of his individual high calibre of work. Note the finned pillars, heavy wheelwork, and the unusual hammer-spring shaped like a musical note.

was used commonly on bracket clocks which might be on a bedside table. The last hour could be ascertained by reaching out and pulling the cord without going to the trouble of striking a light. Sometimes a cord ran from a longcase clock up into the bedroom for the same purpose. Sometimes a longcase repeater was used as a kind of dinner gong to remind those not yet present at table that they should be. A repeating longcase clock involved the use of an extra trigger spring to which the cord was tied.

Longcase repeating was more common in the north than in the south. It is not necessarily a sign of quality, though would not have been put on lesser clocks built down to a lower price. Thirty-hour clocks sometimes had this strike system purely for the purpose of repeating.

Rack strikework is normally located in front of the frontplate (just behind the dial), but sometimes it is between the clock plates; these instances are more often on early forms of it. The essential feature is a stepped cam called a snail, against which the rack tail rests at a greater depth with every hour, thereby allowing the rack itself to drop a greater distance at each successive hour.

One special type of clock is known as a regulator. This was a clock, usually longcase but wall and table examples do exist, made especially for precision timekeeping. A clockmaker would very often make one, or have one made, for his own shop and he would use this like a master clock to test the timekeeping of the clocks he made. It would be known as his 'shop' regulator which would be for use in his workshop or sales shop. Clockmakers vied with one another as to whose regulator kept the best time. Most date from the nineteenth century by which time certain London makers, who specialized in such clocks, might supply one to a provincial maker. So a regulator might be made by the man whose name it bears on its dial, or more likely it would have been made for him.

Regulators usually had separate sub-dials showing seconds, hours, minutes and sometimes a calendar also. The majority had circular single-sheet brass dials, while others had white dials. Most were timepieces, that is they did not have strikework, since the clock's purpose was for precision timekeeping and not for normal domestic use. Many regulators will have special escapements, most commonly a deadbeat escapement, which were perfectly safe for use by an experienced person, but was less satisfactory in household conditions where a variety of different people might be winding the clock. The teeth and pallets of a deadbeat escapement would be more prone to damage from misuse or rough handling.

Many regulators also have a form of maintaining power to keep the clock's wheels turning correctly during winding, thus helping to avoid possible escapement damage. This also had the added benefit of keeping the clock driving during winding so that one did not lose the winding time. Many regulators also had compensated pendulums which could be in any one of many varying forms, and whose purpose was to avoid gain or loss in timekeeping caused by expansion or contraction of the pendulum rod.

Regulators may have been sold to private customers not only to clockmakers. For example, a scientist or an astronomer might want a precision timekeeper. Sometimes public bodies or large company offices might want such a clock, and in these situations accuracy was important. So most regulators are quite large, not having been designed for domestic use. Many have glass-fronted cases to display the particular form of compensated pendulum. Many have very formal, even austere cases. This type of clock is greatly desired by collectors whose interest might be in unusual escapements and accuracy. They are not the kind of clock the average buyer might want, and certainly not the kind of clock a first-time buyer would normally consider. Much of the value of a regulator might be in the escapement and/or pendulum form, and perhaps in its maker if a well-known name.

Regulators were almost always of eight-day duration, or longer. I have had, however, one or two eighteenth-century ones over the years which were clearly the work of the clockmaker himself and which were of thirty-hour duration. The thirty-hour continuous rope (or chain) system is such that a thirty-hour clock does not need maintaining power since perpetual drive is inherent in the system, as long as the clock is kept wound and operates during winding. So for a clockmaker's own premises, where he would be working daily, a thirty-hour regulator was a very sensible idea. Eighteenth-century regulators are uncommon and most of those date from after 1830.

The remarks elsewhere about circular dials and single-sheet brass dials being less popular than other types do not apply to regulators which most commonly have circular single-sheet brass dials (originally silvered over the surface).

3   *Options*

What kind of clock from all those available best fits your needs? Let's have a look at some of the options open to you as a potential buyer of your first clock, or subsequent clocks for that matter. You want the best value for money that you can get, the best buy for you personally, which may not be the best buy at all for someone else. How do you go about it? Where do you start?

Obviously you will have a particular kind of clock in mind. If you fancy a longcase you are unlikely to buy a mantel clock instead. But within the category of your choice will be a vast range of possibilities.

Longcase clocks offer what is probably the widest number of permutations, some of them much more expensive than others. They exist in two basic forms: those you wind once a day, known as thirty-hour clocks, and those you wind once a week, known as eight-day ones. If all other things were equal, which unfortunately in clocks they never are, an eight-day is going to cost you considerably more than a similar thirty-hour. A thirty-hour might typically cost you half to two-thirds of the price of a 'similar' eight-day clock. This is because the clock-buying public at large think that daily winding will be a nuisance and may easily be forgotten. In actual fact it is not. It takes barely two seconds to wind a thirty-hour clock by pulling the rope or chain inside the case. When you have a thirty-hour longcase the winding of it becomes part of the pleasure of ownership, and in practice you are more likely to forget which day to wind an eight-day, than to wind a clock which needs everyday winding.

In the commercial world of clock selling, however, the great majority of buyers are convinced that a thirty-hour will be a nuisance, and they insist on an eight-day. This means that if you are likely to be equally happy with either kind, you will get a much better buy for your money with a thirty-hour. This is good news for thirty-hour enthusiasts. Some people collect nothing but thirty-hour clocks, if you can use the term 'collect' when referring to what might be as few as two or three clocks, because in that field are some truly exciting and interesting clocks, often showing

Ten-inch single-handed longcase by Joseph Norris of Abingdon with birdcage movement. Date about 1700–10. Good quality and a famous name but still a cottage clock.

Pine case of the cottage thirty-hour clock by Joseph Norris of Abingdon. Plus points: tiny height (only 6 ft.), very good condition for pine of this great age, lenticle glass, maker of repute.

a great degree of individual thinking and personality.

Suppose you would particularly like a really old clock, say from the first years of the eighteenth century. No clock of that age is easy to come by. A thirty-hour from that time is quite hard to get, being a rarer survival than a similar eight-day. An eight-day of that age would have been made for a wealthier customer, and a gentleman's goods tend to have been better housed and better cared-for than a cottage item. So, a cottage thirty-hour clock from 1710 is a rare survivor, often very primitively cased in pine or oak, and can be an exciting piece of clockwork, illustrative of the very beginnings of provincial clockmaking. Such a clock can be 'important' in the history of provincial clockmaking, the more so if it happens to have been made in your home county. Yet, in the scale of demand, it is just another thirty-hour clock. If I were to collect clocks myself, that is the sort of clock I would look for.

A thirty-hour pine cottage clock in good order, and dating from say 1700, is a much rarer survivor than an eight-day London walnut or marquetry clock of the same age. If scarcity counted uppermost, the thirty-hour should be far more expensive to buy, but it can be bought for a fraction of the price, perhaps as little as a tenth, of such an eight-day.

Some thirty-hour clocks are single-handers, registering hours and quarters, not minutes. The choice of one hand or two was available from the time the very first longcase clocks were made (roughly 1660) until the beginning of the nineteenth century in some areas, but more generally until about 1760, after which time the single-hander died out slowly. Many single-handers were later modified (spoiled, strictly speaking) to two-handers to keep them in line with the convention of the day. Two hands on a single-handed dial are an obvious giveaway. Surviving single-handed clocks are not rare, but there are fewer of them than two-handers, and they have a certain oddity value today, in so far as our normal habit is now to read the time with two hands. Many a collector and thirty-hour clock enthusiast appreciates a single-handed clock as an interesting form, especially if it is a particularly early one. By rights the single-hander should be quite a bit costlier than the later two-hander. Single-handers, however, do not have such a wide appeal as two-handers, and if they are of modest quality and age, they can often be cheaper than similar two-handers. So, again, this makes single-handed thirty-hour clocks bargain territory for those who care about them.

There is a minus side, however, because overall demand is what matters more than anything else when, if ever, you come to sell your clock. You will find that this inbuilt resistance against thirty-hours goes against you – at least in my twenty-five years in

A group of four oak clocks dating between about 1790 and 1810 with heights ranging from about 6 ft. 10 in. to 7 ft. 2 in. Left to right these are from: Lincs., Co. Durham, Glos. and Lancs.

the trade it always has, and I don't imagine that trend will suddenly change in the next twenty-five.

If you could imagine a graph of prices, which of course are simply a reflection of demand, showing thirty-hour clocks alongside 'similar' eight-day clocks, then the thirty-hour version always runs at half to two-thirds of the level of the eight-day price line, sometimes even less than half. But the two lines do not maintain a constant relationship over the years. You would find that the thirty-hour goes through spells of neglect but, as ever-rising prices creep up, there are times when the relative price level of thirty-hour clocks falls so low against the eight-day level, that they become obvious bargains. At that point, many buyers are drawn to that type by sheer value for money, and the see-saw of relative values begins to swing back the other way.

Things are never quite as straightforward as they might be, and it is obvious on reflection that once a certain price level is passed, thirty-hours fall out of the equation altogether. They were almost always simple and fairly basic cottage clocks. If we get into the higher realms of grander quality eight-day clocks, then there simply are no thirty-hour equivalents. If we think of a grand Lancashire 'Chippendale' mahogany moon-dial longcase, then there are no cottage thirty-hour versions. So prices for thirty-hour clocks reach an ultimate ceiling, whereas eight-days of higher quality keep going further up the scale. At the time of writing this, for instance, very few thirty-hour longcase clocks are selling above the £2,000 level, but a great many eight-days are running well over the £4,000 mark.

So, thirty-hour clocks can be a field of exceptional interest at modest prices, especially if you want to form a small collection. If, however, you want a single clock, you might be more inclined to follow the wider public demand and go for an eight-day. One point about collecting, on whatever scale, is that there comes a point when you must stop, whether for reasons of finance or space. At that time, your collection either remains frozen for ever or else you may decide to upgrade some items by selling and replacing them with eight-day examples. At that point, you are faced with selling your thirty-hour clock(s) into a market still dominated by an eight-day demand.

The thirty-hour/eight-day option exists with longcase clocks, but not with other British clocks. Lantern clocks, for instance, were always of thirty-hour duration. The only time you will see an eight-day one is when it has been much modified by having its movement replaced with a spring-driven (bracket clock) movement so that it can be used on a mantelshelf. English bracket clocks are always of eight-day duration (or longer). Fusee wall clocks are also always eight-day running. The same thing applies to tavern clocks. Hooded clocks are almost always thirty-hours.

Eight days was the standard duration for a longcase clock, but examples do exist that run for a month, three months, six months and a year at one winding. If you want an extra long duration clock, you will have to pay more for the privilege, sometimes much more, simply because they are scarcer. Month-duration clocks are the least uncommon of these longer duration types, but will still cost you more than similar eight-day examples. If you do not especially care about the longer duration factor, then opt for an eight-day and save yourself money. Month-duration clocks were a fashion in London around the turn of the seventeenth/eighteenth centuries, fading out by the 1730s other than for exceptional one-off items made for special customers or special purposes. In the provinces there was never the same call for them, and provincial month-duration clocks tend to crop up here and there throughout the eighteenth century almost at random. Perhaps this is just because a particular maker wanted to try his hand at making one for variety.

In general, eight days was a sensible and satisfactory running time. I had a six-month clock once, which said on its dial: 'Wind me up New Year's Day and Midsummer's Day', and inside the door a log had been kept for the last hundred years or so of dates of winding. In some ways such a clock can be boring because you only get a chance to play with it twice a year. Year-duration clocks are very unusual and have surprisingly delicate escapements and extremely heavy weights, so the cases are usually much sturdier to cope with this stress. Such long-duration clocks are best left to more experienced collectors.

Some features of a clock are normal features of that particular type and do not constitute an extra or a plus factor in terms of price. For instance, eight-day clocks normally have a seconds dial positioned below XII. A longcase usually beats once a second and it is a convenient feature to display. A seconds dial is therefore a normal feature of almost every eight-day clock and such a clock will not cost any more by virtue of its seconds dial.

On the other hand, thirty-hour clocks do not normally have a seconds dial. The wheel in that position on a thirty-hour clock rotates anti-clockwise and, though one does just occasionally see one, an anti-clockwise ticking clock looks odd to say the least. Therefore, a seconds dial was not normal on a thirty-hour. Some, however, do have a clockwise rotating seconds hand, and these have an extra wheel to reverse the direction of turn. Such a thirty-hour clock has a four-wheel train rather than a three-wheel one; a 'train' being the word used in clockwork to signify a set of wheels. A four-wheel thirty-hour is unusual and often a better quality item, which also avoids the 'slop' or play on the hands of a three-wheeler, because the gearing is tighter. A seconds dial on a thirty-hour clock is usually seen as a plus factor in pricing, though only a small one. It may well be, however, a clue to a better quality movement behind the dial.

Some eight-day clocks have what is called a centre seconds hand or a sweep seconds (this is a long seconds hand, usually counter-balanced, i.e. with a tail as well as a point) turning from the dial centre where the main time hands fit. This is unusual, though not rare, and tends to be a plus factor in pricing. A centre-seconds longcase will usually (in fact virtually always) have a deadbeat escapement rather than the normal anchor escapement, because this avoids recoil, which would look exaggeratedly silly on a long hand, but passes unnoticed with a normal seconds hand. So a centre-seconds feature goes together with a deadbeat escapement, being joint factors that add to the price.

The sweep seconds was a feature mostly of north-western England, though they also crop up at random elsewhere. It may look interesting, but has a snag in that you usually have to stop the clock when winding because it is impossible to complete the winding before the sweep hand comes round running the risk of jamming against the winding key. It was a passing phase, occurring mostly in the 1760–80 period, and probably fell out of use because of the nuisance factor during winding, and because in a dimly lit room the multiplicity of hands from the centre made time-reading less easy.

Therefore, when it comes to a seconds dial, sweep or otherwise, does it really matter to you as a buyer whether it one or not? It makes no difference to the price, except when the seconds dial is a sweep type. Are you willing to pay more for the privilege of a sweep seconds dial? If not, opt for one without and save money. An eight-day clock without a seconds dial is unusual and can be a sign of an altered thirty-hour clock (see Chapter 8).

A calendar to show the day of the month was normal on the great majority of longcase clocks. Not every single one has it, but most do. It should not, therefore, make any difference to the price of any clock, thirty-hour or eight-day, whether or not a calendar feature is present. The normal calendar is calibrated to a thirty-one day month; on a month of thirty days or less it has to be pushed on manually to the first, when it will pick up again as usual. A calendar may show through a box (round or square) above VI or just occasionally below XII, or through a mouth-shaped opening, or it may be indicated by a hand. No

Magnificent dial of an eight-day (twelve-inch) longcase by famous maker William Stumbels of Totnes. Date 1740s or a little earlier. A three-train clock but with Stumbels's unique two-winding-square system. (The third train winds anti-clockwise by using the key tail over the shank of the square.) It plays 'Worship the King' or a chime as desired. Ball moon in arch section with lunar and tidal dial. Plus feature: maker's own handwritten instructions for use pasted inside the case!

If you particularly want a clock with a moon dial, it will cost you quite a bit more than that same clock without it. I don't know what proportion of clocks have moons against those that do not, but it is small – perhaps one clock in every twenty or thirty. Clocks with moon dials are usually more sought after than those without, and many people who feel they would like the idea of a moon feature never actually use it or refer to it, and after a few weeks they more or less forget it is there. So, if you would be just as happy without, opt for a clock with no moon and it will save you money.

A moon dial could be positioned anywhere on a clock dial but it commonly takes up the entire arch area when one complete monthly lunar span will be visible. The actual moon disc, of course, covers two lunar months as one half of the disc is always hidden behind the dial. A moon in the arch is usually called a 'rolling moon' and sometimes a moon-dial clock is known as a 'moon roller'. Some clocks, although not many, have a complete ball for a moon, revolving rather than rotating, usually half black and half silvered to show a three-dimensional representation of a moon. This is known as a spherical moon or ball moon, sometimes called a 'Halifax moon', but that latter term is more normally used for a different type. A ball-moon is highly thought of by those who have one, and is very much a plus in terms of price factors. A ball-moon clock is likely to cost you much more than a normal moon-dial, so much so that some clocks, which once had a name disc in the arch, are today being converted by the enterprising into ball-moons to cater for this demand; the ball fits neatly into the existing aperture which makes the conversion easier to fake.

A 'Halifax moon' is usually found on a square-dial clock – often a thirty-hour – being positioned below the XII numeral. It could be a painted or silvered brass moon disc. Generally brass (and silvered) moon discs pre-date painted ones and are rated higher. It is possible for a brass-dial clock to have a moon disc either of silvered brass or a painted disc. A painted dial clock will have only a painted moon disc, not a brass one.

The 'Halifax moon' is often a semi-circular aperture, but sometimes may be circular, when it is usually known as a 'penny moon', often being about the size of an old penny. A 'Halifax moon' is more often found on a thirty-hour clock than on an eight-day, and so is the penny moon version of it.

Almost all moon-dials will show not only the shape of the moon as it appears in the sky (known as the moon's phase) but also a number alongside, which represents the lunar date. Some moon-dials incorporate a tidal dial too, to show 'high water' at a certain port, e.g. Bristol. Occasionally, a tidal dial might carry the name of several different ports, but that is very unusual and will certainly cost you extra. A tidal dial is simply a second scale of numbers around the moon disc. The lunar date runs from 1 to 29½, usually numbered every fifth number. The tidal numbers run from I to XII, usually in Roman numbers to distinguish from the lunar date. This means you can read off, for example, that on the 18th lunar date high water would be at eight o'clock. High water is not quite the same thing as high tide which is when the tide turns. High tide occurs too irregularly to be incorporated into a regularly calibrated disc. High water presumably meant the tide was in and there was enough water to set sail.

Some tidal moon-dials have two pointers as indicators. One is to set for moon reading (usually vertically); the other can be set to read off high water for any port, once a starting point is known. Sometimes, one finds a moon and tidal-dial clock which has been made inland at a town many miles from the sea, and often these have the sort of tidal dial which can be set for any port. There is no particular name for these multi-port types, so I refer to them simply as universal tidal-dials. I often make up names for clock features where no existing term is in regular usage.

A moon dial is an uncommon feature. A tidal dial is even more uncommon and a clock with such a feature will clearly come into a scarcer category and will cost you more. If you don't really want this extra feature, then save money by buying one without it. Would you ever use that feature anyway?

Sometimes, though not often, you may come across a clock which has other indications as well as moons and tides. Some have a zodiacal chart, astrological tables, saints' days, feast days, equation discs (to tell you how much faster or slower to set your clock to mean time from sundial time). All these are unusual features and will add to the price. The dominical letter was used to find out on what day of the week a particular date would fall. The golden number appears on some clocks to give the year position in the nineteen-year cycle of the moon. Some of these items are so complicated that you will need to consult some serious works to understand them, and such clocks are not really within the scope of any but the experienced collector. Just occasionally a clock may have the names of certain foreign countries or cities around the dial, and when the hour hand (or sometimes a special hand with a sun motif) touches those points, it is noon at the designated place. This is known as a world-time-dial clock and these are rare.

Some longcase clocks have a rocking figure, sometimes called an automated figure or a clock with automata, which sounds far grander but is in fact the same thing. This is a very simple mechanical 'extra' on a clock, whereby the figure rocks in unison with the pendulum. The commonest forms are a rocking ship or a rocking Father Time swinging his scythe to reap us all, but other figures do exist such as a swan swimming on a lake, Punch and Judy fighting it out, two people playing badminton, children rocking on a see-saw, a bird hovering in flight and so on. This is the kind of feature you either like or do not. Any rocking figure is uncommon and will add to the price. One of the more unusual versions may well add a considerable premium and the extra cost would only really attract a buyer who was keen on such a combination.

Almost all longcase clocks strike the hour, having one set of gears (known in clock terminology as a train of wheels) for going and another train of wheels for striking. They always strike on bells, or at least they did originally because some were altered in Victorian times to strike on a coiled gong. Gong strikers are almost always modified from bell strikers, except in late Victorian clocks after about 1890 which were built with gongs in Germany for the English market. A non-striking longcase clock has a single train and although unusual, it is generally unpopular in terms of demand. Therefore despite its scarcity, this type of clock might well be less costly than a normal two-train version.

One special category of non-striking longcase clock is a regulator, which was really a clock made for high accuracy of time-keeping, such as a clockmaker might make for his own use in testing his other clocks – a master clock in other words. Unlike a non-striking longcase, a regulator tends to be a costly clock and those who enjoy them revel in the niceties of precision escapements and compensated pendulum systems devised to reduce expansion errors. Usually, a regulator is a non-striker, but it is not the same thing at all as a non-striking longcase.

Some clocks chime on the quarter hour. A simple way of doing that is called ting-tang quarters – usually on two bells, one high-pitched and one low – and such a clock will play one ting-tang at quarter past, two at half past and so on. Other clocks may chime the quarters on several bells – six or eight or even more, usually through a third train. This can be done using the same number of hammers as bells, or using two hammers per bell to allow for rapid succession of the same note. Quarter-chiming clocks will usually strike the hour as well, that is to count out the number of the hour on the hour. Very occasionally a clock which has what is called *grand sonnerie* striking may be discovered, and such a clock chimes the quarter hour followed by the last hour as well. This involves a massive power store and highly skilled work

Lacquer longcase clock by Robert Henderson of Scarborough, height about 7 ft. 10 in., *circa* 1740. The clock has a twelve-inch dial with a rocking Father Time in the arch. Plus pointers: good condition of lacquerwork, good style (pagoda not removed), rocking figure, reputable maker.

in the making and any *grand sonnerie* clock will be costly. Quarter-chiming clocks are rare and costly items and they can be a nuisance to live with as not all have a silencing switch. If complications arise through mechanical wear, they can also be expensive things to repair.

A quarter-chiming longcase clock made before about 1850 is scarce. A great many were made, however, at around the turn of the century – say from about 1870 and later. Many of these later ones were German-made (though made for the English market and possibly lettered on the dial with the name of an English retailer). German quarter-chiming clocks are not at all scarce and are not to be compared in price with an antique British-made one. Most of these German clocks are not of high quality. Even so, the best of these are not usually in the same world as an eighteenth-century English clock which chimes quarters on bells.

Musical longcase clocks are those which play a tune or sometimes a selection of tunes, often hymns or marches. A musical clock will not normally play every hour, but more usually every third or fourth hour. If you have ever lived with one, you may well think that is often enough. Some have a series of seven tunes which will change automatically day by day. Some have manual tune selection. Simpler ones might play on as few as six bells – I doubt if much of a tune can be played on fewer. A cluster of bells on such a clock is known as a 'nest' of bells as they cup one inside the next to save space. Complicated ones can have many bells, twelve, fourteen or even more. Often, they have two hammers per bell for quick note succession. Some clocks even have the tunes named on the dial. A musical clock will usually have three trains, the third train being for the musical drive. Some of these will have a silencing switch.

Inside a musical clock is a barrel, rather like that in a musical box, containing hundreds of pins, each triggering a note from a hammer tail as it passes. Such a barrel that has run for the best part of two hundred years will have been repaired on numerous occasions, sometimes so much so, or so badly, that the tunes can be undecipherable, and these clocks can sometimes play a meaningless jumble of notes. The tune may be one long forgotten and, even if it is named on the dial, you may find it impossible to trace in order to make it play correctly again. It can be impossible to tell which pin marks were trial ones of the maker's doing, or incorrect repairs since removed. Sometimes tune barrels have interchangeable sleeves, each holding perhaps half a dozen tunes. Some were re-sleeved during Victorian times to make the clock play popular tunes of the day. One can of course make it play anything at all by altering the pins. One clock in a famous

A group of later painted dials, mostly of the
1850s, the lower one *circa* 1810.

museum, so the story goes, was during its restoration, for a bit of a joke made to play 'Colonel Bogey'.

A musical clock can become a great mechanical headache and some will never again work as they once did. If you think you would like a musical clock, bear this in mind, as it is likely to cost you dearly in the first place and dearly in repairs, if troublesome.

It is possible to have a clock which plays a tune every few hours *and* chimes the quarters too, which would in fact usually be a *four*-train clock. I had one once and it was fine when I had it, however once I sold it into the hands of a customer, it was nothing but trouble. With such complicated clocks one cannot take liberties. For instance, to move the hands forward without waiting for the appropriate run of chimes or music is a recipe for disaster. This can easily happen if a clock is allowed to run down and an impatient owner unthinkingly forgets. Children, of course, love to mess about with clocks to make them play, and many are mysteriously broken by children who have not been seen doing it. I had that clock back for repair so many times that it taught me a lesson I shall never forget, namely never to buy another. In the hands of a careful collector such a clock is fine because he knows how to handle it, but otherwise …

Do remember, if you are looking for a clock, that the more features you define as essential, the less likely you are ever to find such a combination of things. Remember also that certain functions compete for space on a clock. For instance a moon dial and a rocking figure are both features normally occupying the arch of a dial. If you look for a clock with both features, you will look for a very long time. I have a 'customer' on my requests list who has set his heart on an eighteenth-century London-made brass-dial longcase clock in mahogany with moonwork and quarter chimes and standing less than seven feet six inches. I'm no closer to finding him one now than when he first asked me ten years ago. Whenever I've had a combination of some of these features he has refused it because it did not include all of them. Such a combination is not impossible, but it is very unlikely and I doubt if he will ever buy one.

Within the range of permutations available on longcase clocks certain features may be found in one region more than in others and you need to use this knowledge when determining your choice. For instance, moon-dials were used for night-time travel which was often planned around the time of the full moon so that travellers were able to find their way home. Such a feature was less necessary in towns where there would be some street lighting. There were other reasons for using moon-dials which were associated with farming. The belief was that seeds would

4 Woods, Colours, Shapes and Sizes

One very important factor affecting the value of a clock is the wood its case is made of, and this applies to all clocks except lanterns which have no wooden parts beyond possibly a wall bracket. Other important factors are size, shape, and colour. Add to these variables the permutations involved in its condition and finish (patina, if you like) and you will see that there are endless arrangements of these factors. So in the end every clock is unique in its own right and the range of values and prices can be bewildering to a novice.

It may help, however, if we examine some of these factors, one by one, in an attempt to understand the commercial aspects of clocks. First of all, let us examine types of wood. A longcase clock might be made of pine, oak, walnut, elm, yew, fruitwood, mahogany, rosewood, or a mixture of more than one of these woods. In practice those you will come across are almost always made from the basic four woods: pine, oak, walnut or mahogany. At this stage we are concerned only with the wood that shows, regardless of what timber may have been used in the hidden carcass construction. On many clocks the wood you see *is* the carcass. An oak case, for instance, is oak right through, possibly with softwood glueblocks in the inside corners. Glueblocks could be made of any leftover pieces which would otherwise be wasted, but are commonly pine. Whatever wood the glueblocks are made of has no bearing at all on the value of any clock nor on its age.

The backboards of most clocks are made from either pine or oak. Oak was obviously better, being stronger, and more costly. Pine backboards often got woodworm, oak ones seldom did. London clocks almost always have oak backboards, so do many from Lancashire. Most clocks, however, have pine backs, (though occasionally they are of elm or chestnut). The backboard wood has little or no bearing on value. Obviously oak backboards are preferable. Sometimes backboards have been replaced or extensively restored because of woodworm. A replaced backboard is less desirable than the original one, unless that is very wormy, when a replacement is probably better.

Pine was cheap and readily available (though they sometimes used what was described as Norway pine which was presumably imported). Deal is another name for what we now usually call pine. If you see furniture in pine today you will see what is called stripped pine, waxed pine or white pine, and it is all the same thing, being the raw wood with all its knots and grain showing. It is usually finished with a varnish, hard polish or wax in such a way that its grain and figuring show through. This is the modern treatment which has been fashionable for some good few years now. In the past, however, pine was not used in this way as pine furniture was meant to be covered with paint to hide those very features now thought desirable. Unpainted pine was used for floorboards and sometimes ceilings, but such things as skirting boards, doors, built-in kitchen cupboards were often in pine and were painted over to give them a finish, hide the knots, cover over the nailheads and filler. The same applies to pine clockcases which were painted and often repainted whenever you decorated the house woodwork. Many pine longcases were finished first with a coat of red-lead primer or sometimes blue primer, then painted with gloss paint – green, brown, black, any colour you liked. If you test pine by pressing your thumbnail into a part that does not show, you will make an impress mark. No other wood is that soft.

If you see a stripped pine clock today, it will have had all its coats of different coloured paint removed. This is usually done by dipping the clock in a tank of chemicals.

If you see an old pine case which has not been stripped of its paint, it is almost always a sorry thing. The surface will be blistered, and cracked like a jigsaw because the paint has shrunk. It will also be lumpy if repainted with a dirty brush. Anyone who wishes to keep the 'original' painted surface, under the impression that he is preserving something old, is mistaken or deluding himself. The custom today is to strip them to bare pine, though an owner who felt like repainting his pine case can hardly be accused of doing anything wrong.

It is incorrect to speak of original surface or patina on stripped pine. If any patina exists at all, it is what has accumulated since it was stripped, and that is a fashion of the last thirty years or so and seldom longer. The same applies to colour, as much of the colour in stripped pine will be the varnish, lacquer, polyurethane or wax used on it.

When first stripped, pine will be a whitish-yellow colour, often with remnants of pink or blue base paint which has penetrated the surface here and there. When coated with a liquid sealant or varnish it will accept a wax finish. The colour gradually deepens

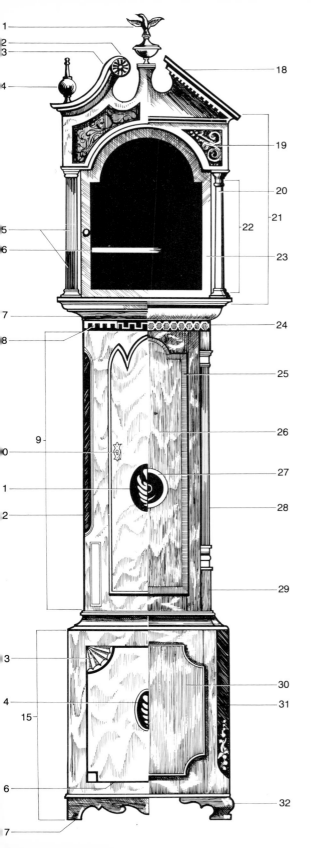

Terms used in describing casework

1 Eagle finial
2 Patera (plural: paterae)
3 Swan neck pediment
4 Spire finial
5 Reeded pillar with double-reeded base
6 Seatboard
7 Top of trunk moulding
8 Dentil moulding (simple left, key pattern right)
9 Trunk or body
10 Escutcheon plate
11 Shell inlay
12 Canted corner
13 Fan inlay
14 Shell inlay
15 Base
16 Stringing Line
17 Plain bracket foot
18 Architectural pediment
19 Blind fretting
20 Plain pillar
21 Hood
22 Pillar caps and bases
23 Hood door
24 Blind fretting
25 Crossbanding
26 Trunk door
27 Lenticle glass
28 Reeded quarter columns
29 Pedestal for quarter column
30 Base panel
31 Canted corner
32 Ogee bracket foot

and after a few years may turn to a honey-coloured shade, which some may prefer to white or whitish-grey. In pine, however, the question of good colour is largely a matter of the preference of the buyer, because the colour factor is not antique anyway.

Sometimes a pine case had flowers or other decorative features painted over the finish colour. Some pine cases were ebonized, that is coated in a fine black polish to simulate ebony. This applies principally to London clocks before about 1730. Some pine cases were originally lacquered, or japanned as it was sometimes termed, and these are dealt with later in the book. Pine was also used as a base wood for cases which were veneered in walnut or mahogany, for example.

Pine is a soft wood which is very prone to rot and woodworm. It is often only the painted finish which preserves a pine case at all. Being soft, a pine case is more likely to be damaged than other woods, especially the base where it has picked up damp from ground contact which would make it even more liable to woodworm attack. A pine case with a replacement base section must therefore be looked upon more leniently than, for instance, an oak case with a replacement base, especially if it is a very early country pine case.

In the two hundred years from 1670 to 1870 inflation did not exist on the scale we know it today, and it is possible to compare prices at some distance apart in this period without this factor confusing the issue unduly. In round figures you could buy a simple pine longcase for 10s. obviously a simple square dial cottage type of pine case. I can think of contemporary prices as low as 8s.6d. A similar oak case would cost £1. Clearly more elaborate examples would be more expensive, but the ratio of pine to oak was roughly half to double. This was for the case alone. The clock itself cost very roughly £3 10s. for a thirty-hour and £5 for an eight-day. So, obviously the whole point of using painted pine was for cheapness, and it follows that it was used mostly for cheaper thirty-hour clocks, though some early cottage eight-day clocks are in pine cases.

Therefore pine was originally equated with cheapness. Today, of course, a very old pine-cased clock can be quite a rarity as so many have been thrown on to the bonfire because of their condition. Thus a pine-cased clock today may be far from cheap, especially if it is well preserved. Pine was used in painted form as late as the 1850s, but by then most cases were of oak and mahogany. Later pine cases tended to be heavier and as pine did not allow the finer detail of working which harder woods did, these later pine cases can be less than elegant.

In terms of values a greater scarcity factor applies to a pine

Ten-inch, two-handed thirty-hour clock by John Fielder of Alton. Note half-hour markers and inner quarter-hour markings to chapter ring, which help date this. Original steel non-matching hands.

Slender and small early oak longcase by John Fielder of Alton, *circa* 1730–40. A very simple cottage clock of only 6 ft. 6 in. Plus factors: sound condition, age, lenticle glass.

clock dating before about 1750, because not only will it have survived longer but the style at that time follows a more simple, slender and graceful theme. A country pine clock may interpret the style of the day in a crude even primitive manner, which constitutes much of its charm. In the end, pine is an acquired taste – either you like it, or you don't. In terms of its original cost, a pine clock should be the lowest on the scale of prices, but today the scarcity factor might override that. Pine often has wormholes somewhere in it, and if these are in a prominent place, for example, the door or the case front, they may well put off buyers. An old pine clock is sure to have worm somewhere – if not, I would be suspicious.

English oak has always been popular from the beginning of longcase clockmaking until the end, though one sees few cases of oak later than 1740 without considerable mahogany trim. Oak could be cut by slicing a log along its length into planks, or by quarter cutting, which involved sawing (or splitting) it into wedges rather like pieces of a cake. The latter was more wasteful but 'better' in many ways. Quarter-cut oak will show better figuring in the form of wavy or snaky lighter patterns called medullary rays. Straight cut oak is very plain grained and can be quite dull or boring as far as figuring is concerned. The primary factor about quarter-cut oak was that it was also less prone to warping. This was especially important if a wide piece was to be used, for example, on a clock door or base panel.

If a single slice of an oak tree were cut wide enough to span an oak case base, then it might well warp, bend, split or tear apart with time, but if several shorter quarter-cut sections were joined together it would not; the more joints the better. If you look at the base of any oak clock you will almost certainly see that it consists of two, three or even more pieces joined together. Joining several quarter-cut pieces was not only better, but obviously costlier as more time and effort went into the making of it.

On many oak cases the quarter-cut timber was used for the parts that showed most and which also covered the widest spans – that is the trunk door and the base section (panelled or otherwise). So it is common to see finely figured oak in these places, whilst the rest of the case can be of straight-sawn (or slash-slawn) and figureless oak. The sides of most oak cases, for instance, seldom show much figure.

The medullary ray figuring was esteemed at the time, and still is by those who like it and know its purpose. A figured case is therefore 'better' and more desirable than a plain, straight-sawn one. Some people, however, have a personal dislike of this figuring, and prefer a plain-grain case which should be cheaper

Eleven-inch eight-day clock by William Tipling
of Leeds, *circa* 1690–1700.

Walnut veneered case (on to pine) of the
Tipling clock. Height about 6 ft. 8 in. Note
barley sugar pillars, bookmatched veneering.
Plus points: age, slender proportions, clean
condition, restrained height.

than a finely figured one – provided you can compare like with like.

Oak was used alone on many clocks until around the 1730s, after which time some smaller areas of other wood were increasingly used for a bit of variety. Fruitwood might have been used for pillars or trunk quarter columns, for instance. Walnut was used for crossbanding, principally on hood door, trunk door, base or base panel. Walnut 'trim', as we describe this for short, may be found as late as the 1750s or 1760s on a good proportion of clocks, after which time mahogany trim was more usual. If you can recognize walnut crossbanding from mahogany (which may not always be easy under layers of dirt and wax) it can be a help in ascertaining the age. Mahogany trim, for instance, almost certainly means the period will be later than the 1750s.

People are often surprised that clock cases were of mixed woods, but it is quite common after the 1770s to find that the majority of oak cases have a greater or lesser amount of mahogany trim; the proportion increasing as time goes by. An 1820s oak clock may have a considerable proportion of the front in mahogany, but not usually the sides, as they didn't show as much. On the wood price scale, however, an oak case is still an oak case even if a large amount of what shows at the front is mahogany, and it only falls into the mahogany price range if it is entirely mahogany.

Oak goes darker with age as layers of dirt are waxed into the surface and become part of the colour. An oak clock of 1710 will be much darker than one of 1810 as some of the early ones are either a near black or very dark brown. This is what should be the case and this darker colour of the earlier clocks is normally considered a desirable feature. This presupposes that the case has not at some time been stripped down. If an oak case is scraped down to the bare surface again, that surface will usually be very much paler in colour and with sanding can become virtually the same as a piece of new oak, with no trace of colour remaining.

Stripping down was done sometimes by an owner who thought he might smarten it up a bit but by doing so unwittingly removed much of its antiquity. Sometimes the surface layer has perished from standing by a window, for instance, where sunlight has cracked the surface and destroyed it. In such cases there may have been little option but to strip off the old polish and start again. Stripped oak is usually yellow, almost the colour of waxed pine. That yellow colour will gradually mellow a little with age and with waxing, and can eventually have a very fine glow of richness which passes for patina. Sometimes a clock has this yellow colour from being stripped down maybe a hundred years ago and can look very fine and have a good deep wax finish. This is usually described as golden oak or honey-coloured oak. It is a fact, however, that most yellow oak cases have been stripped down in fairly recent times.

Older oak will be brown rather than yellow but a whole range of shades are possible. Oak cases were usually stained when first built in order to give them a certain ground colour. Rich browny colours are good. Dead, drab, dirty browns are not. An old finish will have lighter areas which have been well polished, and darker, dirtier areas in the grooves of the mouldings and in parts less easily reached. For instance, the front moulding above the base is the part where pressure can easily be applied, but the sides of that moulding less so. So one would expect to see a wide difference of shades of colour on original finishes according to which parts were easily polishable with a duster. A stripped clock will be of much more uniform colour overall, including awkward corners where you could never really polish in everyday ownership.

Quite often an oak case will be a brown or medium oak colour, but may have a lighter streak down it, running along the grain and often only an inch or so in width. This is a sapwood streak. If oak gets woodworm at all, it will be in this softer, lighter coloured sapwood streak, as oak is otherwise immune to woodworm, unless perhaps in some part softened by damp such as the feet of a clock. The sapwood is the outer part of the tree, closest to the bark, and the part still growing when the tree was felled. This was often discarded, but sometimes a plank would include a sapwood streak, perhaps not noticed during the original sawing, and this always remains lighter than the rest of the wood. Sapwood streaks spoil the appearance of some oak clocks by showing prominently down the door or base.

Does it really matter in the end, if you like it, whether the finish is original or modern, whether it is yellow or brown, or whether it was repolished last week? Well, you will buy what you like in the end, but there is a serious difference and this may well have a bearing on price.

Walnut was an alternative wood available on longcase clocks and bracket clocks from about 1680. Initially it was used in veneered form so that the interesting figurings and patterns could be matched together on the larger surfaces, such as trunk door and base. The patterns were sometimes, indeed often, bookmatched, that is divided at the centre into two reflecting patterns like an open book with two 'matching' pages. A design divided down the door centre is known as halved. It could of course be quartered, or bookmatched down the door in six, eight or more sections.

Walnut was usually veneered on to a pine carcass, because it was thought to adhere better to pine than to oak. Larger areas were veneered, including the sides of the case. Mouldings were usually cut in end grain and jointed in multiple short pieces, as end grain offered a more interesting appearance and polish. Walnut moulds might be cut from the solid wood but faced on to a pine backing.

Sometimes circular grained pieces were selected and whole areas of the case, or even all the case, were made up from these oval pieces, which are called oyster-shells to describe the manner of cutting. These were slices cut at an angle through a branch to produce an oval, or sometimes circular cross section in which the growth rings showed as a pattern. Oyster-shells could be in walnut or indeed any wood and sometimes laburnum or olive-wood was used. An oyster-shell case is likely to be an early one, before say 1720 at the latest, though sometimes a late example turns up. Oyster-shell veneering was costly, labour intensive and such a case is likely to be on a very expensive early clock.

Most walnut cases are bookmatched and have sheet veneers. By 1750 the era of the veneered walnut case had almost ended, though later examples which were made in the 1770s are found today. Walnut was also available in solid form, and a solid walnut case (where of course figuring would be far less spectacular) was no more costly than oak when it was new. Solid walnut cases were a provincial option. Walnut was prone to woodworm and many walnut cases suffered woodworm infestation and have been destroyed. This applied to veneered walnut (on soft pine) and to solid walnut too. Therefore walnut cases are costly today. A veneered one would certainly be costlier than a 'similar' oak case, but would not usually be similar anyway. Solid walnut may have been no dearer originally than oak, and solid walnut cases were more often made in the second half of the eighteenth century (veneered walnut in the first half). Today a solid walnut case ought to be costlier than a similar oak one, but this may not be the case because solid walnut was a plainer wood, plainer indeed than some oak, and may have suffered more from shrinkage warping and woodworm.

So far we have been speaking of English walnut. In veneered form it was usually the fancier figurings (such as curls and busy patterns) that were the attraction. Burr-walnut was the choicest timber as it is highly marked with flecks and swirling grain. English walnut stocks are said to have been exhausted by the 1730s or so. For a time European walnut was supposedly used, but I don't know anyone who can distinguish between European and English. Later in the eighteenth century American walnut was imported. This is a very different wood which we shall look at shortly.

Fine mahogany pagoda-style case housing a clock by William Ward of Grimsby, from about 1790. Plus points: twelve-inch Wilson-style dial with original hands, slender proportions, finest flame mahogany. Height about 7 ft. 10 in.

Walnut veneered cases were costly and would be used only on better quality clocks. Many London clocks from the late seventeenth century until about 1760 were in veneered walnut and these were virtually always eight-day ones. Occasionally provincial eight-day clocks also had such cases and many have been used later to re-house London clocks, which were long thought to be better than provincial ones. Solid cases are not common in English walnut, and it is just as likely that they were for thirty-hour clocks as for eight-day ones because there is little difference in style and quality compared to oak cases of the period.

Parquetry is the name generally given to veneered patterns which are of a simple nature, made up of simple shapes, or large shaped pieces with straight sides. Oyster-shell veneering is a form of parquetry. The sunburst inlays (or compass rose inlays) where alternate light and dark ray lines form a pattern in the groundwood are also parquetry. The term parquetry, however, is normally used where this form of patterned decoration covers a considerable area of the case, or even just the front of the case.

Marquetry is a more extreme version of parquetry, frequently having very complicated and detailed designs of such delicate subjects as flowers, birds, foliage and so on. Two or more sheets of veneer were used to form a design set and several 'sets' were cut at once on a special kind of saw (not unlike a treadle fretsaw in principle) called a 'donkey'. Cutting several sets at once meant not only a saving of time, but made the veneer sheets thicker and less likely to break or tear in cutting. Longcase clocks in marquetry appear from about 1690 to about 1730, after which time the fashion died out save for an occasional throwback. Walnut was the main background wood and many other woods were used in the design detail, such as holly and sycamore. Some woods were stained and are difficult now to identify.

Earlier marquetry clocks tend to be of panel marquetry and these designs are confined to certain sections of the clock only. Later the all-over style followed which was often of flower design. Carnations were favourites along with tulips or roses. Later still came the seaweed style of marquetry which was a much busier style and is sometimes called arabesque. Once you have seen one of each you cannot fail to recognize these styles again.

Marquetry clocks have been desirable for a long time and have probably been faked and copied more than any other kind of clock. A faked marquetry case made a century ago is now old itself and displays many characteristics of the real thing it copied. Telling one from the other is not a beginner's field.

Old marquetry tears as the backing wood (normally oak) moves

A large eight-day 'Yorkshire' clock by J.C. Elliott of Leeds, dating from the 1860s. Height about 8 ft. Negative points: very broad style and heavy proportions, busy dial (though better than some).

or shrinks, and so a clock without any 'shakes' in it is very suspicious. Over the years, little bits are snagged out with polishing and dusting, so old marquetry is likely to have numerous small repairs which usually show. It is an ambition of many clock collectors to own a marquetry example, even though they know this is very treacherous ground. I saw one recently which was very beautiful, but there was not a tear or a shake on it or a sign of a repair anywhere, yet it sold for tens of thousands. Another example at auction not long ago looked to me no older than about 1900 as the wood was slightly dirty, but just too clean to be true. By 'clean' clock dealers mean damage free. The clock it contained was a genuine London clock of about 1700 by nobody of particular repute. After closer examination, I just did not believe it was the three hundred years old it purported to be. You only have to look at a 100-year-old clock to imagine how much greater the wear and tear would be on one which was three hundred years old. Yet dealers from the other end of the land came to this auction and it sold to the trade for over £10,000. I could only conclude that those bidding just didn't know or didn't care whether it was old or not.

Marquetry cases are scarce as many have been destroyed by worm or the passage of time. London clocks (early ones especially) have long been prized more than provincial ones, and numerous provincial clocks that once had marquetry cases have had their cases used on caseless London ones. Therefore marquetry clocks are best left to those with great experience, or courage. A marquetry clock at auction can be a treacherous thing indeed.

Mahogany first came into Britain before the end of the seventeenth century and rare examples of furniture made from it can be quoted from archives in these early years. It was not in general use, however, in clocks until the 1740s, taking over from walnut gradually, and most mahogany cases will date from the 1760s or later. Mahogany came from the West Indies and later from the American mainland. Different islands produced mahoganies of different colours and grains. Sometimes they are called by the island name, such as San Domingo mahogany, Cuban mahogany and so on. Sometimes terms such as Spanish mahogany are used, indicating that the wood is from the Spanish West Indies, not from Spain. There are many different varieties of mahogany and obviously different soils produce different types of growth. The terms Cuban mahogany and Spanish mahogany tend now to be used as generic names for the earlier wood often used in solid form. This is darker in colour, sometimes very dark, and has plainer figuring and a very dense, cold touch almost like steel. So early mahogany clocks can have little figuring and a deep red or red-black colouring, and are mostly of solid wood, including doors and base.

The highly figured and spectacular type of mahogany is sometimes called curl mahogany or crotch mahogany, specifying the type of figuring, not the category of mahogany. The term crotch mahogany is more accurate as these highly figured pieces, often with a balanced pattern, only occurred in the crotch or fork of a tree where two main stems or large branches met. Consequently it was the scarcest bit of the tree and was hard to obtain and highly sought after, especially in larger panels. Some clocks have their doors and base veneered in a matching piece which runs the length of both in a continual pattern. More often door and base pieces are different, but of the same character.

Curl mahogany was always used as a veneer. First of all, it was far too costly to use in the solid. More important, perhaps, was the fact that such busily patterned timber was full of conflicting stresses which were all inclined to pull against each other by nature of the part of the tree it came from. Therefore if it was used in solid form it would have warped, twisted, split or torn apart as a result of its own internal pressures. Mahogany used in the solid, as on a clock door, is always of a much quieter figuring and was chosen to avoid these stresses.

By the 1760s the paler flame-type mahogany, often referred to as Honduras mahogany, was widely in use. Cases then have the overall construction from the solid timber, but the door and base would more often be veneered with a spectacularly figured and sometimes matching panel. Sometimes these were bookmatched as walnut had been. By the early nineteenth century African mahogany was in use. This is more like the mahogany you can buy today as it is pale in colour being a yellow-brown and is altogether an inferior and softer wood. You can whittle African mahogany with a penknife, whereas craftsmen complained that the first Spanish mahoganies were so hard that they used to take the edge off their chisels. Large Victorian clocks are often of African mahogany in the solid parts and this forms a very pale contrast against Spanish mahogany veneered panels which are a deeper, richer colour.

Mahogany had more or less replaced walnut by 1770 and remained in use until the end of clockmaking. It was a very fine and durable wood, sometimes called the king of woods. Some cabinetmakers kept it for ten years to cure before working it. Smiths of Clerkenwell, who made many round fusee wall clocks with mahogany cases in the mid-nineteenth century, kept their timber suspended from the rafters in the heat to dry out for as long as ten years before using. This was to avoid shrinkage after use. In fact, I have a mahogany longcase made in the 1780s with joints as tight as the day they were made with no signs of shrinkage, twisting, pulling, splitting, and certainly no wood-worm because mahogany was immune to worm.

If you think you have seen mahogany furniture with worm holes, it is probably an example of mahogany veneered on to pine. Beetles will eat into the soft pine backboard and will certainly eat their way out through a veneer thickness. Solid Spanish or Honduras mahogany, however, is immune, unless perhaps it has become softened by damp, such as in the feet of a clock.

By the 1820s cheaper versions of mahogany longcases were made and the solid timber was used (unfigured, as the figured was kept for the prominently visible areas) for the sides of the case. Most of the front, however, was veneered on to a pine carcass, in the way walnut had been a century earlier. This form persisted right to the end of longcase making, and after about 1840 the majority of clocks of this type were in mahogany as oak was then much in the minority.

Many people think that a clock in 'solid' mahogany or even 'solid' oak is in some way a better thing. In fact oak was always solid as it was not a wood suitable for veneering (at the periods we are speaking of, that is). So to describe a longcase as 'solid oak' is meaningless since they all are. Mahogany was used in the solid form early in the mahogany period, say 1740 to 1760, after which time the finely-figured frontal parts were almost always veneered. There is no comparison, however, in the quality of work or the timbers if a veneered clock of about 1780 is compared with one of 1840. Therefore it is not the question of veneering or solid which represents quality, but the merits of the individual clock case and the specific wood used.

Mahogany was never a cheap wood. It travelled half way across the world before it could be used. Clocks made of mahogany in the eighteenth and early nineteenth centuries were made for a customer who could afford the best. A mahogany clock case could cost easily £10 or even £15 in the second half of the eighteenth century, when a pine one was still available for ten shillings or a simple oak one for £1. Often, therefore, mahogany was the timber for a gentleman's clock, and he would have had a big house with high ceilings. So many mahogany clocks are grand and tall and may have much inlaid stringing-work, frets or blind frets, fancy carvings and multi-shaped mouldings. Mahogany was seldom used for simple, plain cottage types of clock. Many stand eight feet tall or more and it is not unusual for them to have

Thirty-hour brass dial clock of about 1760 by
Thomas Lister (jun.) of Halifax with twelve
o'clock moon. Original oak case carved and
stained black. Plus features: well-known
maker, moon dial, original brass hands, original
caddy top. Negative points: carving can be
off-putting, somewhat stocky overall
proportions, height about 7 ft. 8 in., thirty-
hour duration.

been in excess of nine feet. Today, many have had protruding bits sawn off to get the height down, especially London clocks. So if you are looking for a cottage clock in mahogany, it is going to be very unlikely that you will find one. A few exist, usually of very mediocre and dull timber, but by and large you are asking for a contradiction of terms.

People sometimes have difficulty distinguishing mahogany from walnut. It is only really difficult when wide areas of veneer are used as on a mahogany bookmatched case, when the figuring and sometimes the pale colour may confuse people into thinking pale mahogany is walnut. Really, walnut was long out of use by this time, so if you see a nineteenth-century veneered clock in what you think is walnut, it is probably faded mahogany.

American walnut is usually called red walnut in Britain, and black walnut in America. This is a stronger wood than English walnut and less prone to worm attack. American walnut can look very like plain-grain mahogany. From about 1760 this wood was used here for longcase making, usually in the solid form. It had a rather richer colour than solid English walnut, which could at times be a pasty grey colour. The grain (not the figuring) is a little stronger than mahogany, but many dealers and collectors confuse the two woods. With a clock of this wood dealers sometimes cut a tiny sliver off the inside where it does not show (such as the inside of the door) in order to see the actual colour of the raw wood, since the surface colour has two centuries of wax and discolouration. Walnut will show a brown colour and mahogany a distinct red. Red walnut is sometimes thought of as being a scarcer wood than mahogany and may be priced into a higher bracket by those trying to sell one. In practice there is little difference between this and a plainer, medium-coloured mahogany one, as far as desirability is concerned.

Elm was occasionally used for clock casemaking, principally for cases of cheaper cottage clocks. Elm cases were very often, if not always, painted like pine ones, and many elm cases show faint traces of paint, indicating that they have been stripped down, perhaps long ago. Elm is very prone to woodworm. Chestnut looks very like oak but is also very prone to woodworm. I have never seen a chestnut case, but it was often used for backboards. If it looks like oak and has woodworm, it's probably chestnut, but the backboard timber in any case has no bearing on the value of a clock. Yew was seldom used for longcase clocks. I doubt if I've ever seen more than two or three examples. It can be a handsome wood in certain pieces of furniture, but in large areas such as a clockcase, it is prone to shrinking, warping, splitting, curling and tearing, which is probably why it was hardly ever used. The ones

I have seen have certainly suffered badly. Large planks of yew were seldom available which may be another reason why few clock cases were made from this.

Fruitwood is the name used for any fruit wood timber, but principally apple. It was used on cottage cases sometimes, but was very prone to worm. Fruitwood can have a very good colour and polish, where it survives in reasonable condition, but this is seldom. It usually has little in the way of figuring. More often fruitwood can be dull and drab. Its comparative scarcity should place it in the higher price reaches, but in fact fruitwood cases are usually modest country clocks of no great quality or style, even verging on the primitive at times. Oak mostly does the same job better and a good oak country case probably beats a modest fruitwood example. Fruitwood can be confused with solid walnut. I don't know anyone who can distinguish one fruit from another on a 200-year-old clock.

Japanning or lacquering is the name given to a particular style adopted in London from about 1690, though mostly found in the 1730 to 1770 period. In the provinces lacquer cases were copying the fashionable London style of the day and, in fact, many provincial clocks in lacquer cases are in London-made cases which were bought in from the capital when the clock was first made so as to keep up with the times. It is doubtful whether many, if any, provincial cabinetmakers could have made a living making lacquered cases.

I have a blue lacquered longcase by a Scarborough maker, Robert Henderson, which is in its original, but London-made, case and dates from about 1740. Its London origin is obvious by its style anyway, but common sense alone would ask the question: who could have made lacquered clockcases in Scarborough in 1740? It was not general practice for provincial clockmakers to buy their clock cases from London, though it did happen now and then and probably by specific request of the customer who perhaps wanted the newest and most fashionable style of the day. I had a clock some years ago of about 1700 by John Sanderson of Wigton in a lacquer case which presumably came from London because at that time they were only just beginning to make clocks in Wigton and nobody there at that time could have had the stylistic or technical knowledge to have made a lacquer case.

Oddly enough, both John Sanderson and Robert Henderson were Quakers and, by chance, Henderson was born not ten miles from Wigton. The Quaker principles were towards simplicity and lack of ostentation and it is difficult to think of anything so contrary to those principles as lacquer. So here again common sense alone indicates that these cases were the specific choice of the customer. Many clocks were made to order and the shape, size, style and wood used would have been dictated by the customer himself, possibly with recommendations on the part of the clockmaker or cabinetmaker to assist. The cabinetmaker's drawings and price-lists which survive from Gillows of Lancaster, few though they are, show the principle very well. What happened was that they quoted a price for the case based on the style and timber, and then added as extras every bit of crossbanding, stringing, inlay, carving or other 'trim' based on a price of so much per foot extra.

Lacquered cases were usually of pine construction, with the exception of the trunk door and possible exception of the base front panel and hood door, which were of oak. On the trunk door and base panel (sometimes the hood door too) the lacquerwork is raised into three dimensions by multiple layers of gums; a very time-consuming business. The decorative colours were then applied over this raised surface, but were put directly on to the rest of the case. Some older books tell us that this work was done in the Far East and that completed (raw wood) cases were shipped over there for treatment and shipped back several years later. I don't believe this personally, as it makes nonsense in terms of logistics, commercial factors and time, and I don't think a single documented example has been found of this happening to a clockcase. Some books tell us that just the doors were sent. I think this is a misinterpretation of the fact that lacquer case doors are in oak while the rest is usually in pine. Oddly enough the backboards are usually oak too, but that was general practice on most London cases of whatever wood.

Lacquer deteriorates with age, where wood finishes usually improve. The commonest problem is that the finish is destroyed by heat, sunlight, damp or excessive changes in temperature, and after 200 years many are in a pathetic condition. Feeble attempts have often been made to brighten up the paintwork, usually with disastrous results. Today there are expert restorers who can do a proper job, but this is not cheap and in the end you have a new, even if 'antiqued' finish, which to my mind is not something most people look for in an antique. Many examples cropping up today in auctions are in a very bad state. At the time of writing this it is possible to buy a poor one at auction for £600 to £1,000, where a respectable example of a lacquer clock by even a modest maker will bring not less than £2,000 and often much more. This is a measure of the poor general regard for distressed examples.

The most common colour is black, followed by green or blue, red, and then yellow; the latter being very scarce. Lacquer is an

Large all-mahogany eight-day clock by Probert of Wigan, dating from about 1790 and standing about 7 ft. 10 in. Plus points: rolling moon, first period dial of good quality and well-restored, much use of inlay in the form of shells and stringing, clean condition. Negative points: fourteen-inch dial, very broad.

acquired taste. Either you like it or you don't. Consequently it is not universally a good selling style as it appeals to a limited market. It is not generally a style which appeals to a beginner.

Rosewood was used sparingly because of its expense and is mostly seen as small veneered sections on clocks of late Regency or Victorian age. It was sometimes used in crossbanding on clocks of a slightly earlier period. Bracket clocks were made from this and so were some fusee wall clocks, always in veneered form. I can only recall ever seeing one British longcase that was entirely of rosewood and that was a grotesque Gothic monstrosity made at great cost and with great skill, but it *was* ugly. Walnut is, in fact, sometimes mistaken for rosewood.

It is perhaps helpful in assessing the age of a clock if you can recognize the wood the case is made of. Does the wood itself, however, have a bearing on the price or value of the clock? Well yes, but only to a limited extent, as other factors combine with the wood to make a clock highly desirable or unsaleable.

Pine appeals only to devotees of pine and in some ways it is in a world of its own. We can forget lesser woods such as fruitwood, elm and even solid walnut (in English cottage case form), as these timbers will only really be used on country clock cases of a similar type, often thirty-hours, and in the scale of prices will roughly equate with oak anyway. English veneered walnut cases are obviously of a considerable age (pre 1760 and perhaps as old as 1680) so sheer survival rate alone puts them into a scarcer category than some other woods. Also veneered walnut was used on better quality clocks; a second factor which puts these into a higher plane. So a good walnut veneered clock will almost certainly be an eight-day, probably a town or city clock (especially London), and these factors will rate it above oak on any comparative scale. Such a walnut clock may well outrate a mahogany one, but we are not really comparing similar items.

From 1750 mahogany reigned supreme for grander clocks, solid or veneered. Mahogany from the second half of the eighteenth century will probably cost more than anything else if you compare like objects, but seldom is any mahogany clock stylistically like any oak one. As the nineteenth century progressed, and especially after about 1830, mahogany was used on virtually all longcase clocks, but the framework was now pine and the quality and style was poorer.

Therefore, after about 1830, the fact that a case is made of mahogany should not really make any difference to price, since by this time they all are. Most will also be of the type veneered on to a pine structure and will be of a lower quality. A few later ones, however, with pine substructure are very fine clocks.

So woods themselves are important, provided you can recognize them. If you can't, then whenever you look at a clock ask what the wood is, and you soon will pick it up. There is no great mystery about it and you will only need to learn to distinguish four basic woods from each other. The timber used, however, is in the end only one factor of many. The others include quality, age, condition, colour and size, and these points are examined later in the book.

5   Other Weight-driven Clocks

Lantern clocks were made in England from the late sixteenth century, though seldom today are we likely to come across one made before the 1660s. These were sometimes called Cromwellian clocks and occasionally still are. Nobody knows why because in Cromwell's day they were the *only* clocks. This situation changed, however, with the coming of the pendulum just before 1660, and it is possible that after 1660 this type was looked on as old-fashioned; the kind of clock to have originated in Cromwell's time, rather as we might today refer back to things which are pre-war.

The first lantern clocks were obviously made without a pendulum and were regulated by a balance-wheel; a circular wheel which rotated to and fro above the movement with its pace acting as an interrupter gear to the escapement. Balance-wheel clocks were less accurate as time-keepers than pendulum ones. They were regulated by adding to or removing lead shot from the weight canister – the heavier the weight, the faster the clock ran. It was not unknown for them to vary by a quarter of an hour a day, whereas the new (from 1660) verge pendulum was accurate to within a few minutes a day. Therefore, almost without exception, balance-wheel clocks were converted to the new pendulum system, either shortly after 1660 or some years after. It is a matter of discussion whether *any* lantern clock survives today with its original balance-wheel. Most of those that have balance-wheel control do so because they have been re-converted from the modified pendulum form *back* to balance-wheel.

The first form of pendulum was a short pendulum, about six inches long, and is called a verge pendulum, a bob pendulum, or sometimes a short pendulum. This latter term, however, is ambiguous as it might refer to other forms of short pendulum, though we know what it means when expressly used in relation to a lantern clock.

A new kind of pendulum control was devised in the late 1670s, and by the 1680s, or a little later, was coming into wide use on longcase clocks. This was called the long pendulum as it was in

Full size lantern clock signed 'James Delaunce in Froome fecit', about 1690. The external frame, finials and feet are very fine and of unusual style. Modified in the nineteenth century to double-fusee movement. The keyholes are cut through the original engraving. The hour hand could well be original, but the minute hand was added later on conversion. Fine engraving, full of boldness and character. Blank centre zone within scribe circle would have been covered by an alarm disc. Note practice engraved flower below 'fecit', once hidden by alarm disc.

A very good striking lantern clock made in 1692 by Richard Savage of Shrewsbury, signed 'Richard Savage fecitt 1692'. Front fret signed 'Edw. Mill. Pardo'. The first owner, Edward Pardo, married Milborough Browne in 1692. Probably a wedding clock. Good engraving, original hand, and original condition throughout. Date and owner's name are plus factors.

Movement of the Richard Savage lantern clock showing original wheelwork throughout. Original verge pendulum positioned unusually inside the iron backplate. The top and bottom plates are also in iron which is very uncommon.

the region of three feet long. A one-second pendulum length is 39.14 inches (99.42 cms), but by no means all long pendulums beat at exactly one-second intervals. The long pendulum (anciently called the Royal pendulum) was controlled by the anchor escapement. The greater accuracy this gave meant that time-keeping could be controlled within a minute or two a week.

The close succession of the verge pendulum followed by the long (anchor) pendulum meant that any balance-wheel lantern clock could have been modified to improve its time-keeping by converting either to verge, direct to anchor, or even through one form to the other.

If this sounds dauntingly complicated to the beginner, take consolation in the fact that it is to the experienced as well. Most lantern clocks one sees today will have long pendulum control. They might have been built originally with long pendulum, verge, or balance-wheel. To recognize them, one has to study empty (or filled) holes in order to determine what has been moved from where. To complicate matters further, a clock modified from balance-wheel, or verge to anchor, might in more recent times have been converted back again in the course of restoration to its original form of escapement. To try to attempt to figure all this out in the viewing time at an auction or in an antique shop is no mean feat. Pondering over it for a day with the required books to hand is a different matter.

There are, however, yet more factors to be taken into consideration. Lantern clocks were originally wound once a day and some even twice a day. As time went by, they became increasingly obsolete. Those which were not modified by conversion to anchor escapement were often scrapped or relegated to the clockmaker's junk box. By the mid nineteenth century there was a certain interest in these clocks as objects of antiquity, and some of these old 'scrapped' lantern clocks were brought up to date by removing all the interior wheelwork and bars and fitting instead a double-fusee spring-driven movement, such as those used in bracket clocks. This might have been a discarded bracket clock movement or one purpose-built for the job. Usually the fitting of an old bracket clock movement meant drilling the dial centre with two winding-holes, which was a pity as it spoilt the dial engraving pattern. Those who made a spring movement would often construct them so that they could be wound from the back, thereby avoiding disfigurement of the dial.

A fusee lantern conversion would run for eight days (like a bracket clock) and could be used on the mantelshelf or table-top. With such a clock it is often the case that the outside 'box' might date from perhaps 1690, whilst the whole of the inside might date from 1860. (Of course some reproduction models were built *new* with a double-fusee movement). Technically such a converted clock has been spoiled and until recently they were very much looked down on. As the prices of genuine lantern clocks have escalated, however, these fusee-conversion forms have begun to come into their own as being one affordable way a less affluent buyer can own one. A fusee-conversion lantern clock could be half the price of an average original and maybe less than a quarter of the price of a good original.

With lantern clocks the fact that the escapement may have been modified later – to verge, anchor, or back to a former type – is not regarded as damning the clock. It is seen more as a normal and natural part of its life over the last two or three hundred years. An older conversion is seen as being 'better' than a more recent one. For instance, a verge lantern clock of 1660 modified to anchor in 1690 is rated better than one modified to anchor in 1800. This is because the modification itself has a certain antiquarian interest. Some were even modified to the 'new' time-keeping control by the actual maker of the clock himself. Many more are claimed by dealers to have been later modified by the maker, often on flimsy evidence. But such modification was so common that it is regarded today by collectors as normal. Conversion to fusee however is quite a different thing and fusee-converted lanterns are in a lower category of their own in the price scale.

Original examples with original (unconverted) balance-wheel control are so rare they are believed not to exist, though sometimes it is claimed that they do. Original examples with original verge escapement do exist, but are hard to come by and would certainly rate higher in the price scale than a 'similar' anchor-converted clock, or a similar 'original anchor' model. Models with original anchor are the most common of any unmodified type. The position of those re-converted in recent times back to their original form of escapement is open to debate and opinion. Some collectors would prefer a re-conversion to one modified and not re-converted, and some would not!

One indication which can help is the position of the hammer. Lantern clocks wound with a continuous rope (post 1660) have the hammer on the left and are pendulum clocks. Those with right-hand hammers probably had two separate weights and probably were balance-wheel ones originally.

By now you will have gathered why I said earlier that lanterns were not really clocks for beginners. Even some dealers, who are experienced at other kinds of clocks, are terrified of lanterns. There is even more reason for this, however, than the complications of conversions and re-conversions. Many of these

Transitional form of lantern clock made by Walter Archer of Stow-on-the-Wold about 1720. His dial engraving is bold and imaginative and distinctly recognizable by his style. The hand is original.

Movement of the Walter Archer clock showing hook and spikes, dominant use of iron rather than brass, original anchor escapement, and original wooden weight-pulley.

Dial of ten-inch Quaker zig-zag style dating from about 1740, not signed (in the Quaker tradition). This dial is, in fact, made of copper with a pewter chapter ring and lead spandrels – a very unusual combination. Its style locates it to Oxfordshire. The movement is a posted hook-and-spike type. Plus features: all the aforementioned aspects. Negative features: none, provided you like clocksmith work.

old lantern clocks, abandoned in former times to the scrap box, have since been revived by taking bits of several to make up into one whole. Many today are made-up or made as outright fakes, sometimes using some old parts or reproduction castings which are produced today for restoring original clocks with missing parts. So, given that most 'original' lanterns have been altered, lost parts or had parts replaced, and given that these compete in today's market for shelf space with made-up examples and outright fakes, it is small wonder buyers have great reservations about the whole field of lantern clocks.

Many genuine lantern clocks have lost their brass side doors or have had them replaced with new ones. This is partly because of the loose way these doors just clipped into place. Missing or replaced doors are such a common occurrence that this is not regarded as any great detriment to the clock and would not put off a serious buyer. The same applies to the backplate of the clock which was normally of iron, but has often been replaced later by a brass one or may be missing altogether.

The frets on a lantern clock screw into place, each with two screws. Original screws often have a square head, but fakers know that and can make a square-headed screw when they want to. Again, the frets of many original clocks are sometimes missing and sometimes replaced, and this is not usually regarded as an off-putting factor. Many lantern clocks, however, had the maker's name engraved on the front fret, and this was often the only means of identification. If that 'signed' front fret is a fake, a modern fret with a 'genuine' name engraved cleverly on to it or a genuine named fret from some other clock (or from a scrap box), then the clock bearing it was made by some other, unidentified maker! So buyers are, or should be, particularly wary of clocks signed on the fret.

Many lantern clocks were originally sold without a name and are still in that form today. Some of these are very fine and highly desirable items. The preference for named clocks rather than unsigned ones, however, has meant that some, once without names, mysteriously acquire them! It is not only fret-signed clocks that have signatures faked on to them. Some signed on the dial-plate might have an insignificant name erased and a 'better' name engraved there instead. If you can buy a lantern clock by John Doe at £2,000 and convincingly alter the name to Thomas Tompion, you might easily double or treble your money. I happen to keep a card index of every lantern clock I have come across for the last twenty years or so, and it is surprising how many 'Tompion' ones fail to sell at auction and how some sell at a 'bargain' price such as £600.

Therefore, because of the high proportion of suspect lantern clocks, the normal rules of clock buying operate in this field in reverse. It is probably much safer to buy one unsigned or by some lesser known or even unrecorded maker, than one by a 'good' maker.

There is a very large and detailed book (539 pages) on lantern clocks called *English Lantern Clocks* by George White, published in 1989 by the Antique Collectors' Club. It is not light reading, but if you want to know about lantern clocks, that is the book to read.

Lantern clocks were made in three sizes. The normal height is about 15 inches though some are only 10 inches and others are miniatures standing about 6 inches high. The smaller types are scarcer and more inclined to be travelling alarm clocks (i.e. without strikework). By 1700 some lantern clocks had a square dial rather like a small longcase dial in shape, but only perhaps 6 or 8 inches wide. By the mid eighteenth century some had a miniature arched dial. Even as late as the 1760s some of these were still being made (originally) with the short pendulum, because of the convenience when moving it from place to place.

Prices vary greatly because of condition and modification, as well as the basic type. In general, it is impossible to buy any real English lantern clock under £1,500 and few today will start under £2,000. A good one may be two or three times that price.

Some were made for the Turkish market and have 'Turkish' numbers. These are generally rated lower than more usual types. A fusee conversion usually rates around half the price of a basic average example. French ones do turn up, but are less liked and cheaper.

If you buy a lantern your best bet is to go to someone who understands them and can begin to explain to you its various pendulum modifications, and probably anything else you want to know about it.

The lantern clock went through a variety of forms including some of a 'transitional' nature. Some of these developed towards becoming a certain kind of thirty-hour longcase clock, even though the longcase had begun life as a fully fledged form from its beginning in 1658. Some thirty-hour longcases were really only square-dial forms of lantern clock without the rear hoop and spurs, from which a lantern normally hung on the wall. Some lantern clocks however went in the direction of becoming hook-and-spike clocks; that is a clock which hung from the wall like a lantern, but whose pillars became simpler and whose fancy finials, frets, side doors and so on were regarded as unnecessary. Hook-and-spike clocks were really cheap and simple forms of the cottage hanging wall clock. Good ones are relatively scarce and

Typical posted movement of a thirty-hour hook-and-spike clock,
mid eighteenth century.

Thirty-hour hooded wall clock by Robert Croome of Wotton-under-Edge, Glos., dating from about 1765. We can date this closely as the maker worked from 1762 till he died young in 1768. Dial about six inches square. The hood is of pine, painted kitchen green, and has no glass. The clock has alarmwork and no strikework. Engraving good but conventional. Original hand.

some are extremely attractive in a primitive way. Quite often they had alarm work.

Some hook-and-spike forms were used on the wall and then, perhaps when the owners could save a bit more money, were housed into long cases, where occasionally they were hung on the backboard rather than sited on the normal seatboard.

Some developed into a form known as the hooded clock which is, in essence, a form of lantern clock sitting on a shelf and surrounded by a wooden cover to keep out dust. Those which had alarm work were usually non-striking as they would be used within earshot of the bedroom. Some were of posted construction, like a lantern movement but simpler. Others, especially later ones, had plated movements like a thirty-hour longcase. Hooded clocks were often simple affairs made for a cottage customer who could not afford anything pretentious. Many had simple hoods of pine, but some were oak or plain solid walnut. Many pine hoods were destroyed by woodworm, and today some have replacement hoods or sit on modern brackets.

It was the dials, and sometimes the movements, of such hooded clocks that were often used to make up grandmother clocks in later times. It is impossible to generalize about prices of hooded wall clocks or hook-and-spike clocks as they vary greatly. However until recently they have been considerably less expensive than true lantern clocks, though not usually as old of course, and they have for the most part been far less subject to faking.

Another kind of weight-driven clock is the type sometimes called an Act of Parliament clock, after the act of 1797 which imposed a tax on watches. Its effect on the watch trade was so disastrous that it virtually destroyed the watchmaking industry before it was repealed only nine months later. The origin of the name was that because this tax stopped watch sales dead, this caused a greater demand for public clocks, such as these large-dialled wooden wall clocks sited in taverns and public buildings. The theory does not hold true though, since these tavern clocks, as they are more correctly called, were on sale for half a century before the tax they are supposed to be named after.

The dials of tavern clocks are made of joined planks of wood which often show from shrinkage, with no glass dial cover. They can be as wide as thirty inches and the clocks can reach a height of six feet, even though they are wall-mounted. Those who see a picture in a book and imagine they might like one are usually astonished when they see one in the flesh to find how massive they are. They are a bit large for the sitting-room wall. They are also rather costly things, because they seem never to have been

Full size tavern clock of the shield dial type, dating from the mid eighteenth century, japanned in black with gold decoration. Five-wheel train running eight days in a short drop. Height about 5 ft. 6 in.

Weight-driven wall clock, sometimes called a Norfolk clock, but really a smaller form of tavern clock, running eight days in short drop. The maker is Richard Francis of Wymondham in Norfolk, and the year of making is known from an inscription inside the case reading: 'S. Wright bot. this time piece of Mr. Francis Sep 14 1812'. This is a white dial. The case is oak and just under 4 feet. Twelve-inch dial.

commonplace clocks and today they are very scarce. They were especially uncommon in northern areas; the majority surviving are southern in origin and a high proportion of these are London clocks.

Tavern clocks were mostly non-striking with a single train of wheels and an extra wheel to give eight-day duration in a short drop. The painted wooden dials (mostly black although occasionally white) stand open to the atmosphere and are often discoloured from years of firesmoke and nicotine. One can imagine such a clock looking very handsome in the large room of an old coaching inn, where the time could be seen by all across the length of the room.

Most cases were lacquered, generally in black, but sometimes in other colours such as blue or green. Sometimes they turn up at auction in appalling condition, having been rescued from some forgotten loft or pub cellar. Even in poor condition, these clocks can seldom be bought for less than £3,000, and some will run much higher. A superb one by the right maker could bring nearer £10,000. Personally I find it difficult to see the value in them in relation to what that amount of money would purchase in a longcase clock.

Tavern clocks are very much an acquired taste. They are more likely to appeal to an experienced collector than to a beginner. Tavern clocks are difficult to examine properly at auction because of their sheer size and the difficulty of getting the dial off to look at the movement. Fakes are made today which look convincingly dirty and old with shrunken timbers being used for the dial boards, just like the real thing. These fakes are mostly offered through auction where people may buy them despite being unable to examine the movement.

A smaller type of weight-driven wall clock, which might also be called a tavern clock, is more often known as a 'Norfolk' clock – whether or not made in that county. These might have a dial thirteen inches across or thereabouts (usually a circular japanned dial) and a total case height of perhaps three to four feet. They have a glass door to protect the dial. The cases are often in mahogany, although some are in oak. Dials are usually Birmingham white dials, like those on some longcase clocks or spring-dial clocks. Some have a single-sheet silvered dial and, occasionally, they may have a deadbeat escapement and maintaining power. The finer ones were probably used in offices and public buildings, such as banks. This type of smaller tavern clock is perhaps best called by some other name, even if Norfolk clock seems inappropriate. These also run eight days in a short drop. Prices of these are modest than those of true tavern clocks and much depends on style and elegance. Some can be bought under £1,000, although the usual price is between £1,000 and £2,000. It is difficult, however, to imagine even a very fine one reaching £3,000. The book to read about tavern clocks is *English Dial Clocks* by Ronald Rose.

6 Spring Clocks

Springmaking was a difficult art to perfect. Most clockmakers could not make springs, but bought them from specialist springmakers. Spring-driven clocks always have the inherent problem that the pulling power weakens as the spring runs down, whereas weights pull at a consistent rate. The fusee gear was an attempt at solving this problem in England. Even so, spring clocks were always more difficult to make than weight clocks, were less reliable at time-keeping, more delicate, perhaps even more temperamental, and were likely to stand up less well to the hazards of daily life, at a time when household conditions were far less clean than today. For these reasons, spring clocks in their early days were almost exclusively the property of the wealthy.

A simple weight-driven clock was sturdier and cheaper. It rang out the hours on a loud bell which could be heard all round the house, for the average weight clock owner was unlikely to have more than a single clock in the house during the seventeenth century and in the less affluent sections of society until the end of the nineteenth. The bell of a table clock was quieter because the owner of such a clock would probably have more than one clock in the house. A table clock was also portable by virtue of its size. Most early ones have carrying handles. It could, if one so wished, be carried upstairs at night to sit on the bedside table where a loud bell would have been unwelcome. Some table clocks therefore have a silencing switch to cut out the strike at night. Some have alarmwork instead. Others have a repeating cord whereby the nearest hour could be established during darkness simply by reaching out of bed to trigger the repeat without all the fuss involved in striking a light.

Spring-driven table clocks are usually called bracket clocks, even though only a small proportion of them ever had wall brackets on which they could be mounted. They were used either on a large mantel or a table. Many have beautifully engraved backplates, a fashion which lasted till the end of the eighteenth century. The fine backplate engraving was visible through the

Ebonized bracket clock, single train with pull-wind alarmwork (setting dial in the arch) and pull-repeat facility on two bells, standing sixteen inches tall. Maker Joseph Antram, watch & clock maker to King George I. Date about 1720. Plus points: prestigious maker, original verge escapement, alarm and pull-repeat are extra value points, engraved and signed backplate.

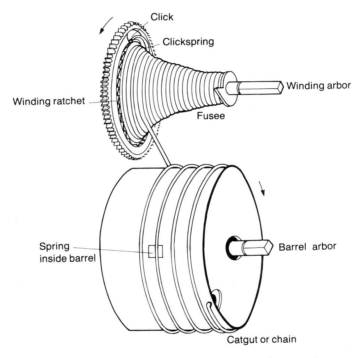

Click

Clickspring

Winding arbor

Winding ratchet

Fusee

Spring
inside barrel

Barrel arbor

Catgut or chain

The fusee principle: arrow indicates direction of turn when running

glass door at the rear of the clock, which suggests they were displayed on a mantel, which had a large mirror behind, thus reflecting the backplate. On a table, of course, the engraving could be seen as one passed by.

Early ones had the verge escapement with a short (bob) pendulum. Some early longcases had verge escapements as well as some lanterns, but the long pendulum soon replaced it in these kinds of clocks. Bracket clocks, however, retained the verge for much longer. Most bracket clocks were made with verge escapements until the last few years of the eighteenth century, long after the anchor was well tried and tested. The reason was that the verge was far less fussy about being on a level surface. You can pick up a running verge clock and move it from one table to another without it stopping; something which is impossible with an anchor escapement and, in any case, may cause damage. By the last years of the eighteenth century, however, the superior time-keeping abilities of the anchor escapement meant that the verge became obsolete.

Many verge-escapement bracket clocks were later modified to anchor to improve time-keeping. This happened particularly in the second half of the nineteenth century when new clocks were made with anchor and a whole generation of clockmakers had grown up with its superior time-keeping properties. They often felt that they could greatly improve an old-fashioned verge clock by converting it to the better escapement system, as they saw it, and they did so with no regard to the fact that they were despoiling craftsmanship that might be well over a century old. Victorian clockmaker Benjamin Vulliamy, a clockmaker revered today by collectors, is on record as having removed a complete movement by Thomas Tompion, the 'father of English clockmaking', and substituted it with one of his own making, because he knew he could make a better one. This is akin to our removing the movements of antique clocks and replacing them with quartz ones today. Most of us don't do that because we are concerned to preserve a clock as an antique item. Converting verge bracket clocks to anchor, however, was seen in Victorian times as an improvement.

A collector today naturally prefers to buy one with original verge which will always be worth more than a similar one which has been converted to anchor. A collector would probably not be dissuaded from buying one which was an anchor conversion if he liked the clock anyway, but he would probably far prefer to buy an original verge version if he could find one. With those which have been converted to anchor there are two choices. They can be left as they are accepting that this was a natural part of the life of many a bracket clock. Or they can be re-converted to verge, restoring the clock to the way it was originally. Different views are held about this. With a re-conversion you are replacing parts which might be 150 years old with new ones and re-converting a verge escapement is quite a costly business. In terms of price, a re-converted verge probably beats the same clock left in a converted anchor state, and many collectors accept the re-conversion as inevitable. They do, however, generally like to know if the verge is original or a replacement.

Therefore, when speaking of bracket clocks with verge escapement, one generally refers to it as 'original' verge or 'reconverted' verge to distinguish between the two. The rub is that after some years a re-conversion which was well done may be very hard to distinguish from original work. A beginner is unlikely to recognize one from the other, and many an experienced collector could not either – unless the movement were removed or taken apart (an opportunity not always available at the time of inspection with a view to buying).

The anchor escapement was, as we know, in use by the late seventeenth century, but it was the late eighteenth century before it was common on bracket clocks. It is probably because the verge is known to be the older form that verge escapement bracket clocks tend to be prized above anchor ones (original anchor that is). After 1800 nearly all bracket clocks had anchor escapements.

Most of the bracket clocks you see today are London-made and carry a London name on the dial. That name could be the maker or the retailer. Often it will be a retailer, even with older clocks from the eighteenth century. Provincial ones do exist, and most of them will date from the nineteenth century when provincial makers or retailers may have bought them in from London, ready lettered with their own name.

London-named clocks may also have been bought from a specialist spring clockmaker. This was a practice far more widespread than is sometimes realized. There were London concerns who specialized in the making of spring clocks – bracket clocks and wall types also. One such concern was Thwaites & Reed which was a company of several generations founded in the 1740s by one of the Thwaites family.

The Thwaites 'factory' made spring clocks for many clockmakers, including those with 'famous' London names. Some of their business records survive today, including certain lists of serial numbers from which a Thwaites-made clock can sometimes be dated to the actual year. Ronald Rose, in his excellent book *English Dial Clocks*, lists some of these serial numbers and, if you are hoping to date a Thwaites-made clock, this is the book you

Mahogany bracket clock *circa* 1840 by George Lee of Skipton, inlaid with brass. Height about eighteen inches with two-train, double-fusee, anchor escapement.

Three-train bracket clock in rosewood with brass inlay made in 1837 by William Grant of London. Height twenty-two inches. Chiming quarter-hours on six bells. Plus points: multiple bell chime, rosewood plus brass inlay, good maker (or retailer?)

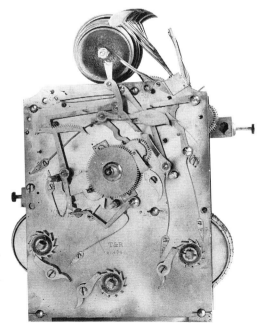

Frontplate of quarter-chiming bracket clock by William Grant showing complexity of work normally hidden by dial. The stamp T & R on the frontplate followed by a reference number indicates that the movement was made by Thwaites & Reed, specialist spring clockmakers, and the number dates this to 1837.

Single fusee skeleton clock with passing strike (one blow at each hour), mid-nineteenth century, anchor escapement, dome removed for photograph. Typical of many of the simpler forms. (picture courtesy Charles Taylor)

will need. Rose also lists some of the London makers for whom Thwaites made spring clocks. Thwaites were only one of the spring clockmaking specialists. So with many bracket clocks it is more likely they will be centrally made by such a specialist, than by the man whose name is on the dial. Such a specialist-made clock is not always easy to identify as not all are marked. They can be recognized, if at all, by the standardized shape of the plates, bell-hammer and so on. An individual clockmaker would be more likely to vary these, thus displaying his own original styling.

In practical terms it makes little difference, as a bracket clock will sell on its own merits, whether made by the person whose name appears on the dial or by a central 'wholesaler'. If your interest is in local clockmaking, then one made locally, rather than simply sold there, would obviously appeal more provided you can recognize it as such.

Bracket clocks are influenced in price by the same factors as longcases. Dial styles follow the same trends and can be dated just as easily as longcase dials. The size is a very important factor also. Generally speaking, small is very much more desirable than large.

The average English bracket clocks stand about twenty inches high (plus or minus two inches for the carrying handle or finial). Smaller examples exist at around the ten to twelve inch mark. More complex or more showy models can be larger, especially those which do complicated mechanical things such as play fourteen tunes. The smaller ones are often timepieces, i.e. non-striking. A two-train will outrate a similar single-train model. A three-train will outrate others, except perhaps a four-train which would be very unusual.

Age and smallness raise the price considerably. After 1820 bracket clocks are more common, and most examples a beginner sees will fall into the 1820–60 period and will have circular white dials.

Early examples were often ebonized, but some were walnut and occasionally marquetry or japanned ones are met with. Of these, black is the least sought after, and marquetry probably the costliest – just in case terms. Much more, however, depends on age and the maker when dealing with early clocks. After 1770 many were made in mahogany and continued to be made in this type of wood right up to the end of bracket clockmaking, with a fashion for rosewood examples in the 1830s and 1840s. If you were comparing like items, then rosewood probably outrates mahogany.

Another kind of bracket clock was the skeleton clock. This is, in principle, only a bracket clock without a wooden case as its plates are made in a fanciful form with fretted areas so that the whole of the wheelwork can be seen as the clock runs. Skeleton clocks mostly date from the beginning of the nineteenth century, but the majority seen will be from mid century. They occur as simple single-fusee models or with two, three or even four trains. Those with more than two trains were often made very large and had their plates in the form of, for instance, a cathedral with spires. Most had a glass cover when new, though many have been broken over the years and now stand open to the atmosphere and dust. Others have a replacement glass dome. Those with original domes are obviously preferred, and a wrong dome will often be given away by its different shape, wrong height and so on. The skeleton clock movement is interesting as the fusee system, concealed on most bracket clocks, is in full view. Skeleton clocks are a bit of an acquired taste. They are not usually a first-time buyer's clock. This is not because they are difficult to understand, but simply because they appeal more to a collector who already may have more conventional clocks. *Skeleton Clocks* by F.B. Royer-Collard will give you much more information on this type.

A simple single-fusee skeleton clock might be bought between about £500 and £1,000, according to its style and condition. Double or triple fusee models can rise to much higher levels, especially if of a very large or complex nature such as the cathedral models.

Earlier spring clocks were table or mantel models. It was not really until well into the eighteenth century that wall clocks were made for domestic use using spring movements. These were normally single-train clocks and were, in effect, like a bracket clock movement and had the same sort of verge escapement as bracket clocks until the anchor escapement took over towards the end of the eighteenth century. Because of their late appearance on the scene as a general type, spring wall clocks with verge escapement (unaltered to anchor or re-converted) are uncommon and are therefore expensive. In outward appearance they look vaguely like the ordinary round dial wall clock, typical of a school clock or station clock. There are considerable differences in detail, but what might vaguely look like a school clock to a beginner can be a very much older and scarcer object if it is a verge model. A round-dial wall clock with verge escapement will usually have a brass dial and it is unlikely today that you would buy a good one under £2,000. One that is more unusual or by a better maker could well cost much more.

On the other hand, a simple school clock of mid nineteenth-century origin or later could well be bought for £200 or £300 (full restoration could increase that, of course). Oak was the

Round dial single fusee wall clock by Rhodes & Son, Bradford, mid nineteenth century. This one is in mahogany with a flat twelve-inch dial.

Single fusee wall clock of drop-dial type in mahogany made about 1840 by Hancock & Son, Yeovil. Thirteen-inch convex dial (and glass). Plus points: drop-dial type, pendulum window edged with brass bead, brass inlay to curved base section, gadrooned earpieces.

commonest wood for such cheaper clocks. Better ones were in mahogany which today will cost quite a bit more than oak – perhaps from £300 upwards. There is quite a variety of quality in even these simple round-dial clocks which might, to a beginner, look much the same as each other, but which in practice are not the same thing at all.

Most English dial clocks, as these are called, are non-strikers. This was probably because they were primarily for time-telling, but without the striking mechanism the price was able to be kept down. In some situations these were used in public buildings, such as banks or offices, where striking would have been thought to be a distraction. Striking versions are uncommon and inevitably more costly.

Somewhat grander versions of the spring-dial clock were made, and these have a projection below the circular section in the form of a box, in which the somewhat longer pendulum hangs. Most 'drop dials', as these are called, have a small window in the front of the box area to view the swinging pendulum bob. Most drop dials also have 'ears' (small carved or gadrooned earpieces) which stylistically join the square box to the round part of the clock. The ears were prone to damage and on some clocks these may have been removed instead of repaired.

Most drop-dial clocks were made of mahogany, although some were in oak. In Regency times a number were in rosewood. Grander examples were inlaid with brass or mother-of-pearl decoration.

In general, dial clocks have dials of twelve, thirteen or fourteen inches in diameter (although the latter is less common). A few have dials of only ten or even eight inches in diameter and the smaller ones are more sought after and more costly. A drop dial usually comes into a higher price range than a simple circular wall clock. Any clean drop-dial clock will probably cost a minimum of £400 today, but better quality and rarer features will take many to a higher price level.

Anyone interested in this type of clock should read Ronald Rose's excellent and detailed book *English Dial Clocks*, when some idea of the great variety of styles and complexities of the subject will be appreciated. These simple round-dial clocks were made into the 1930s and were used on railway platforms, RAF barracks and the like. These later ones are very common, less sought after and consequently probably much cheaper. The fusee models are quite good time-keepers despite their age. It's only a few years ago that I bought the one which had hung in our local police station probably since it was made in the 1890s.

7   Who Made the Clock and Does it Matter?

The question often uppermost in the mind of a potential buyer is: who actually made the clock? Any clock was the work of more than one man, but when we refer to the 'maker' we usually mean the person whose name is on the dial.

With a longcase clock, the maker made the clock movement and, with many brass-dial clocks, the dial too. Painted (white) dials were a specialist product which the clockmaker bought to put on his clock according to the fashionable style of the day. The clockcase was made by a cabinetmaker, specialist clockcase maker, carpenter or joiner according to the location and quality. So with any longcase clock the whole item was the work of two or maybe three different craftsmen. The man who organized it all, made the mechanics, assembled the final product, found the customer for it and sold it, was the one we refer to as the clock's maker and it is his name which appears on the dial.

A lantern clock was usually made in its entirety by the man named on its dial or fret, though of course sometimes he may have been a retailer buying the clock ready-made with his name lettered on it as the seller. Spring-driven clocks (fusee wall clocks and bracket clocks) were rather different in that these clocks were to a great extent the product of London specialist clockmaking concerns. Many spring clocks therefore carry what is really the name of the retailer, even though that retailer may have been a very capable maker himself of weight-driven clocks. The making of spring clocks was an art for which most clockmakers were not equipped, and as spring clocks were costlier than other kinds and less accurate as time-keepers, they were items forming a very much smaller portion of the normal trade of most clockmakers, especially of provincial clockmakers.

So the infrequent demand for these meant that it was hardly worthwhile for most clockmakers to develop the skills and the equipment for making them. Most spring clocks then were London-made for a retailer, though some were made by the retailer himself. It is very difficult to tell one from the other and, by and large, makes no difference to the price. Some London specialist makers did leave a trade mark on a clock movement and in these examples the actual makers can be identified. This is dealt with more fully under the section on spring clocks (Chapter 6).

Suppose you have seen a clock which you are considering buying and you want to know more about the maker. Was the clock made by a real clockmaker or is the name on the dial simply a retailer? Was he a good, famous or completely unknown clockmaker, and are these factors important anyway? Does the name tell you anything ultimately? Where do you look up information to aid you in your agonizing decision? If you are a novice, then what you are looking for really is moral support, something in writing to back up your hunch that the one you have taken a fancy to is a 'good' clock. Because although you are little more than a bemused stranger on the shore of horology, you feel that by some inner sixth sense you will recognize a good thing when you see it. Where can you turn for support, for confirmation in the wisdom of your selection and for extra information?

First of all, if the clock is being sold by a dealer, you should ask him everything you want to know. That after all is what he is there for. He is an expert, so he should be able to answer all your questions. Try him out first and see how you get on. Most dealers in clocks do have a fairly good idea what they are about, and are only too pleased to answer your questions and demonstrate the finer points of their clock and their knowledge. If they can't, then that in itself speaks louder than words and you should ask yourself why you are even considering buying it from him. Therefore a dealer who knows what he's doing can answer all your questions, including the idiotic ones which might wear his good nature a bit thin.

The ones who don't know will waffle or tell you a pack of lies. It is amazing the imaginative stories I've heard told about clocks – the ones that formerly belonged to famous personalities, second cousins of royalty, or impoverished gentry – which are usually without the slightest shred of evidence. Some antique dealers have such fertile imaginations that they would make good novelists. In a shop one day I overheard the owner offering an American watch to a 'victim', as he used to call his potential customers. It was an amazing story about how it was 'supposed to have belonged to' a Confederate officer in the American Civil War who fell on hard times, and on it went till I had to go outside to dry my eyes. Later I asked how the dealer knew all this, and he explained that he didn't actually *know* that, but it was an American watch and it might well have done. I asked why a

All-mahogany clock with much inlay and stringing work made about 1810 by John Chambley of Wolverhampton. Plus points: much brasswork and all original, good dial painting, clean condition, good proportions and balance. Height 7 ft. 10 in.

Confederate officer and not a Union one, and he explained that people always sympathize with the underdogs, and as the Confederates lost the war, that was where his best chance lay.

This was an interesting lesson in psychology. He didn't actually say the clock had belonged to a Confederate officer, but only that it was 'supposed to have', thus removing from himself any obligation of proof in what was purely a story he had invented. At the same time, however, he sowed the seeds of historic and romantic association in the mind of the gullible victim. The dealer was no doubt a keen student of auction catalogues. A seasoned buyer learns to totally ignore any fairy tales unless they are signed, sealed and written in blood.

Let us suppose, however, you are contrary enough to want to buy a clock from someone who doesn't know what he is selling (or pretends not to). How do you check on the maker's details? Was he a clockmaker or retailer, for instance.

The first place to look up any clockmaker's name is in the bible of the trade, called *Watchmakers and Clockmakers of the World* by G.H., Baillie. This is a compilation of one-line entries on roughly 35,000 clockmakers which was first published in 1929 and reprinted many times since although unchanged since the 1940s. Mr Baillie died many years ago and in 1976 I compiled a further list of clockmakers either absent from 'Baillie' (as this book is known for short) or about whom more facts had since come to light. My listing was increased and revised again in a new edition in 1989 and now contains roughly 40,000 entries. The two volumes are now referred to as Volume One (by Baillie) and Volume Two (by myself) and contain brief facts on over 70,000 clockmakers. They sell as a twin pack (published by NAG Press) and you need both volumes. It was not possible for copyright reasons to simply up-date Volume One and sell it as a single volume, which in any case would have been almost 700 pages. The period covered is from the earliest times to about 1880, and if you are looking for a clockmaker who worked within the last 100 years, you will not find him there. So 'Baillie' I & II is the likeliest place to trace any clockmaker (or retailer). Clockmakers still come to light, however, who are not recorded here.

If the name you are seeking is not recorded in 'Baillie' (or indeed anywhere else) does that matter? Does it mean the clock is a fake, by some insignificant retailer or in some way inferior? What it means principally is that the compilers of lists (and they've been compiling them since 1894) have so far failed to come across that name. This may simply be a failing on the part of the compilers and not on the part of the clockmaker. The usual reason for such an omission is that he may have been a

Exceptional all-mahogany clock of about 1790 by D. Robb of Montrose. Plus factors: small height (about 7 ft.), original finials, slender proportions, clean condition, twelve-inch dial of first period (Wilson type), rolling moonwork, original hands.

lesser-known clockmaker, perhaps from some remote country area, or one who was in business for a relatively short time and has therefore left fewer clocks behind him. He may have been a superb craftsman who simply happens to have gone unrecorded. On the other hand, it may be a faked or invented name. Some old reproduction clocks were given invented names to give the impression of age. Water clocks, for instance, often bear such quaint names as 'William Smythe in ye old towne of Yorke', and may fool you until you learn that all water clocks are all modern. In the end, all you can deduce by the failure of a name to appear in any reference lists is that it has escaped being recorded, and it should not imply any dubiousness about the clock itself. In fact, people react strangely to unrecorded names and are usually much happier to buy a clock by a name that is 'in the book'.

Your second port of call in researching a name should be Britten's *Old Clocks & Watches and Their Makers*, first published in 1894. Its list of 14,000 makers was of limited use, but the latest edition of 1982, as revised by Cecil Clutton and published by Methuen, contains an extended list of 25,000 makers up to 1875. Most of the entries are also in Baillie, but the new Britten is strong on London makers, often giving details of apprenticeship.

British clockmakers who were working by the year 1700 (but not those who commenced later than that) are documented in as much detail as possible in *The Early Clockmakers of Great Britain* by myself and published by NAG Press, 1982.

For Scottish makers the only work of reference is John Smith's *Old Scottish Clockmakers* published in 1921. Welsh makers are set out in *Clock and Watch Makers in Wales* by Iorweth C. Peate published in 1960. These two books may well give greater detail on makers already documented in Baillie, but are unlikely to include makers not already in Baillie.

Studies have been published on the clockmakers of certain towns and counties – the old counties naturally, not the present administrative areas. If you are lucky then the county of your maker might be amongst them. County books tend not to be commercially viable from a publisher's point of view today, and it is unlikely that any more will be published in the near future.

Towns which have been covered individually are:
Birmingham, Chester, Colchester, Dunfermline, Exeter, Hamilton, Hull (& East Riding), Leamington (with Warwick), Nantwich, Salisbury (with part of Wiltshire), Stamford, Stirling, Tiverton, Warwick (with Leamington).

Counties covered individually are:

Buckinghamshire, Cornwall, Cumberland, Derbyshire, Devonshire, Dorset, Durham (with Northumberland), Gloucestershire, Lancashire, Lanarkshire, Leicestershire, Oxfordshire, Northumberland (with Durham), Nottinghamshire, Shropshire, Somerset, Sussex, Warwickshire, Westmorland, Wiltshire (part of), Yorkshire.

These titles are all set out fully with publishers in the bibliography. Some are large publishers but others are small private presses amounting to no more than the author financing his own book, and may be hard to find today. Many are now out of print, but the libraries should either have them or be able to locate a copy for you.

Supposing, however, you try all the books of names and fail to find the one you want. Well, your next place to turn to is to the reference books on clock styles, though bear in mind that these books are written to explain styles and how they have developed with time. They are not intended to contain reference lists of clockmakers, though obviously if your maker happens by chance to be mentioned in one of these books, then you may find some information about him and, if you are lucky, an illustrated example of one of his clocks. This may then enable you to make a comparison with the one you have seen.

You will need to consult books on style if you intend to go any further as you will need some idea of the approximate age of the clock and ideally the region. Both of these factors can be established by reference to a good book on clock styles – the more detailed the better. A considerable selection of such books appears in the bibliography. Use a modern book if you can as there is little point in going out into today's clock market armed with knowledge that is fifty years old because knowledge, opinions and attitudes have changed considerably in that time.

Most signatures on clock dials include the maker's town or village. If the one you want to investigate is not recorded in the standard books and names no town, then you are in trouble, as you don't even know in what part of the country to begin. Although you may be able to find this information in the dictionaries of makers mentioned above. Assuming you have the town you can try writing to the local library or museum, though they seldom have any facts on makers not documented in the books mentioned earlier.

More likely you will have to try in these cases to investigate the maker for yourself which will involve the amateur detective work of genealogy, visiting the local County Record Office and studying parish registers and wills. If you are persistent and lucky, you may well uncover some facts about the maker. This sort of research is enjoyable in its own right and is the sort of thing you might have great fun doing *after* you have bought your clock. Whether you have time to do this in the interval, between first viewing a clock and making up your mind to buy, is very doubtful.

You will more than likely find something about the maker in a book such as Baillie. In fact most people who sell clocks will have looked it up already and be able to refer you to the actual entry. You still don't know, however, whether the name on the dial was the maker or merely a retailer. If he was a retailer, then the actual maker of the clock may remain for ever unknown as it is unlikely to be recorded anywhere inside the clock movement.

How *do* you tell whether the name is that of the maker or retailer? Let's take a longcase example. An expert can tell immediately in those cases where it is obvious, and so can you. First of all, let's take those cases where you cannot easily tell. If it's any consolation, the 'expert' cannot tell in these cases either, at least very few can. In fact, the expert is doing little more than guessing, and you can guess just as easily as he can by knowing the general trend.

Most makers of weight-driven clocks made their own clocks from the earliest times. Even rustic and isolated craftsmen (sometimes called clocksmiths) whose work is of a simple and primitive nature did their own work. They simply could not afford to buy in ready-made clocks to re-sell as that was too expensive. By the early nineteenth century the situation began to change, but it was not till about 1830 that a clockmaker could easily buy in ready-made sets of clockwork which were rather like do-it-yourself kits. The clockmaker of the 1830s (and later) increasingly became a clock finisher (at the time known as a 'clock dresser'), putting the finishing touches to the wheelwork and assembling. So it's a fair guess that those clocks made before 1830 are likely to have been made by the man whose name is on the dial, and those after will not.

By this date all longcase clocks had painted dials (with the exception that the single-sheet brass dial was still occasionally used in parts of the south-west and Scotland, and in more general use as a round dial). Until about 1830 most painted-dial longcase clocks (never brass dials) had the dial fitted by means of a falseplate which began to fall from use after that time. The presence of a falseplate (on a clock which has not been modified later, of course) is in very general terms likely to be an indicator that its movement was made by the local man and not by some sort of 'factory'. This is only a broad indicator and is not an infallible rule.

Eight-day all-mahogany clock of about 1790 by
John Hunter of Bridlington, standing about 7 ft.
10 in. Plus points: fine condition, rolling moon,
best style of Wilson period dial with additional
flower swags, not too tall.

In those instances where you *can* easily distinguish one from the other, it can usually be seen that the clockmaker himself would have marked out the plate for locating the positions for his wheels. Often circles were scribed on, i.e. scratched with dividers into the brass surface. Some clock plates were polished and filed up to give a pleasing finish. The front of the frontplate (that area which you would be facing if the dial were removed) showed least when the clock was in a fully assembled state, and that was the area which was often *not* filed or polished, so that the scribe lines would still be visible today. The front of the frontplate is a bit tricky to see when the dial is in place – you have to try to glance at it from the side (for which a torch is a help). If you make the effort, you will usually be able to see the scribe lines quite well, and that is an indication that the clock was hand-made by the man whose name is on the dial.

Therefore with longcase clocks, anything before 1800 or a little later was almost certainly made by the man himself or his workmen (who were known as journeymen). Just occasionally he might have had another clockmaker construct a specially compli-cated clock for him if the work called for was outside his normal parameters, but here we are speaking of complex items such as musical clocks.

Does it really matter whether the clock you like the look of was actually made by the man whose name is on the dial or assembled by him? Well, by and large it does not. If he was a retailer then the clock is likely to be after 1830 and may fall within the category of later clocks, where quality was lower than earlier. Therefore this indication of later age and lower quality may help you. Most people, however, who buy a clock would not be put off because it was made by a retailer rather than a maker, even if they knew that or thought to ask about it. If you are seeking an early example of handcraftsmanship, then obviously this would matter to you, and for that reason you will need to learn how to recognize it.

Then there is the question of famous names. Is he a famous maker or not? Much depends on how famous. If he is one of the top dozen or so clockmakers of all time, such as Thomas Tompion, Joseph Knibb, Daniel Quare or Ahasuerus Fromanteel, then the person selling it will certainly know that and will probably be able to show you considerable reference documentation about the maker. For £30,000 or so you would expect that.

The top price that I know of for a longcase clock was one by Tompion sold in July 1989 in Christie's London rooms at £880,000 (plus VAT of £12,000!). If you want to buy a clock in that sort of price range, you'd better go to someone who can tell you every detail of Tompion's life and recognize every Tompion screw and wheel – and such people are few.

Each county had its top twenty makers with often one or two who stood out from all the rest. You can only learn who these were by studying enough books on the subject until eventually the best-known names will become second nature to you. Once again, if the maker is of some repute then the vendor will know that and can tell you some facts about him and where to read up on his work. Fame, however, is not the same thing as good craftsmanship and many an excellent clock was produced by a maker about whom little if anything is known.

There is also a considerable amount of silliness about 'good' names, as well as misunderstanding which is mostly propagated by those trying to sell a clock who hype up the name of the maker of the clock they hope to sell. Even makers whose names are well thought of, such as Thomas Ogden, Henry Hindley and the two Thomas Listers would make clocks to a lower price when a cheaper clock was called for. Many a simple thirty-hour clock by such makers may be no better or worse than a thousand similar clocks by makers who may be unheard of. Even run-of-the-mill eight-day clocks by them can be quite ordinary, and in those cases what you are paying extra for is purely the name. The supposition is that you are necessarily buying a 'better' clock because it bears a well-known name, but this may not be the case.

To make matters more confusing, false nameplates have long been put on to other clocks to give the impression that they are by well-known makers. I can think of at least five eight-day clocks I have seen in the last ten years signed 'Henry Hindley, York', which were not by Hindley at all, but simply have false nameplates. I can think of a painted dial longcase lettered 'Jonas Barber, Winster' which brought an astonishing price at auction, but which Barber never saw in his life. With painted dials it is very easy to add a false name.

Fortunately some of these 'better' makers had their own idiosyncratic ways of doing things and the experienced can recognize any Barber or Hindley clock by its internal features. So if you are thinking of buying a clock by some supposedly 'good' maker, the best thing is to ask the vendor to point out those features by which it can be identified as a genuine clock by that man. Also ask him in which books you can read about his individual work style and, if the vendor can't refer you to such a book, ask him how he comes to have that knowledge. Remember that talk is cheap and you can very soon find yourself in the land of the Confederate watch.

How *do* you recognize quality when you see it? We've already looked at dial quality. Quality in movements is a more mysterious thing and is measured to a large extent by the amount of extra work a maker put into his clock, when less would have functioned just as well. Busily turned pillars (sometimes known as 'finned' pillars), shaped plates and decorative hammer-springs are the sorts of things which are, to a large degree, a measure of age. This is because older clocks often have these whereas in later clocks they were dropped as being unnecessary. Certainly they are a measure of quality, but clocks of 1720 would usually have them as a normal part of clockwork, and clocks of 1820 would not. The reason for this was that the custom of the day was to go for greater simplicity in an effort to keep prices lower in the face of greater competition. This is why an earlier clock is often thought of as being superior to a later one, even though both may function equally well in mechanical terms.

Movement quality is a difficult field for a beginner, and is more a matter of judging well-cut wheels and crisp engineering work. If a clock is said to be of high quality in terms of its movement, then why not ask the vendor what that means and ask him to point out to you those features which reveal it?

When checking names on dials, you will find that many painted dial clocks have dials which have been worn by wet-cloth cleaning in the past and appear now to have no maker's name. A great many of these appear in auction catalogues as nameless clocks. Very often it is possible to decipher the dial name on inspection, especially if you develop the knack of doing this. It is mostly only a matter of getting a glimpse of the worn name in the right light and at the right angle. You may find the same thing applies to clocks you see in dealers' shops. If you can read a name the vendor can't, this may be an added incentive for you to buy that clock.

Bear in mind, however, that many auctioneers suffer from dyslexia. Just glancing back at a few past catalogues on my desk I noticed the following names: Peter Borver of Redlynch, Emanuel Copperton of Leeds, Smorthmail of Colchester, Thomas Shan of Lancaster, J. Wilton of Peterborough, Thomas Listel of Halifax, Tom Hardy, Larpeth. You would never find those in any book of names because they are careless misreading of names on dials, which correctly are: Peter Bower, Emanuel Hopperton, Smorth-waite, Thomas Shaw, J. Wilson, Thomas Lister and John Hardy of Morpeth. These are all real examples from recent catalogues.

Another more unusual one, which I found quite puzzling at first, was a painted dial, 'the arch painted with Bums and Muse'. You would not find these listed as an archaic partnership in any book, and if it referred to objects in the painted scenes, they would be unusual to say the least. Eventually I realized the clock showed Robert *Burns* inspired by the Muse of poetry! Not long

Detail on the hood and dial of the clock by William Sully of Langport, dating 1830–40. Plus points: restrained style, original hands and brasswork, good condition, shaped backsplats echoing pillar shapes, restrained dial decoration.

Eight-day oak-case clock with mahogany crossbanding by William Sully of Langport, Somerset made about 1830–40. Plus factors: small height (only 6 ft. 6 in.), clean condition, good styling and shaping to hood pillars and swan neck.

ago I was offered a clock on the phone and when I asked the maker's name I was told it was 'Soli & Co., Gloria'. What sounded at first like a very unusual name of a Jewish clockmaking concern in Transylvania proved to be a Latin motto 'Soli deo Gloria', meaning 'glory to the one and only God'. So do read the name for yourself or your researching efforts may prove fruitless.

Sometimes clocks are signed, but do not have any placename. This was more likely to happen in a smaller country hamlet, the name of which might not be known some twenty miles distant. A typical example of this was clockmaker Will Snow who worked only a couple of miles from where I live at a hamlet called Padside, which in the mid-eighteenth century probably consisted of four houses. As it happened, this clockmaker numbered each clock he made, so he would sign it, for example 'Will Snow 661'. Just occasionally he would include the placename, but mostly he did not. I had to smile one time when a well-meaning correspondent wrote to tell me that he had finally found out which house Will Snow worked at as he had seen a clock with his full address: 'Will Snow, 56, Padside'. He had mistaken Padside for a street name!

One reason makers in smaller villages often failed to put any placename on the dial was that they might well attend regular markets at some distance from home and take their clocks along to sell them (probably without cases). In those instances a placename on the dial would have 'committed' them to one location. There is the famous case of John Sanderson, the Quaker clockmaker from Wigton in Cumberland, who was fined in 1715 for selling his wares as far away as at Edinburgh. He was prosecuted because he did not belong to the local guild whose members had exclusive rights to trade there.

Even though the placename might not appear on the dial, many of these places are known today, and can be located by looking up the clockmaker's name in the appropriate books.

Sometimes a clock was signed (with or without a placename) including the word 'fecit'. This simply means 'made it'. It was felt that this added a certain dignity and pride to the work, and 'fecit' was used mostly on earlier clocks before about 1730. Occasionally it appeared later, however, and I saw it recently on a painted-dial clock of about 1790 which is most unusually late. This word is sometimes misunderstood. I recall seeing a record of a clock by Thomas Lister of 'Luddenden Thicket'. Now Luddenden is a hamlet near Halifax where the Listers did live and work, but local historians must have scratched their heads pondering where on earth Luddenden Thicket was, when it must have been a misreading of 'Luddenden Fecit'!

Some clocks are not signed at all, and these can present a bit of a puzzle. Many will never be identified and the reasons for them being nameless are not known. Some nameless clocks are so because they were made up (as 'marriages') using old bits and pieces and no nameplate was available. Others, however, are quite genuine and still nameless. One possible reason is that they may have been made by a blacksmith or whitesmith, a skilled metalworker but not a trained clockmaker who maybe felt he should not, as a 'professional', put his name on a clock. One sometimes reads in books about a law that was passed obliging clockmakers to sign their work. This is in fact incorrect. It was not a law applying nationally, but only to the clockmakers who worked in London and was done to prevent anyone working there who was not a member of the Clockmakers' Company – the guild which had authority over the craft in London *only*.

Sometimes dealers will describe a clockmaker as being a Member of the Clockmakers' Company as if it was some sign of merit. It was in the sense that if the Company did not regard his work as of high enough standard they would not admit him. On the other hand, anyone who worked at the trade in London was *obliged* to join, not as an honour, but like a compulsory 'closed shop'. Therefore provincial clockmakers did not fall within the Company's sphere of control and provincial makers were not, as a result, members (with the exception that a handful were admitted in the late eighteenth century as a special concession, perhaps to allow them to sell some of their products in the capital).

Amongst those clocks which are unsigned will be a number made by Quaker clockmakers. The Quaker ethic was to be self-effacing. When one died he would leave nothing behind by which he might be remembered, as that was regarded as a sign of vanity. For this reason many Quakers did not even erect tombstones. To sign one's name on a clock was thus thought of as vanity by those who held their beliefs strongest. Many Quaker clockmakers, however, did sign their clocks just like non-Quakers.

If a clock is unsigned, how can you tell whether it is a Quaker clock or not? The answer in brief is that you probably can't. There are one or two localities where Quaker styling was very strong and can be recognized. Certain Quaker clockmakers in part of Oxfordshire, for instance, used a very eccentric style which is easily recognized once you have seen it, because the dial centre design consists of a series of concentric circles interspersed with radiating lines. This style is known as a 'zig-zag' dial, and various permutations of it exist by certain Oxfordshire Quaker clockmakers (some known and some unknown) who are principally of the Gilkes family.

Quaker work in other areas sometimes has distinctive features to it and, when these appear on an unsigned dial, they *may* be a clue that it is Quaker work. Some Quakers for example did not use corner spandrels on brass dials. Quakers went in for sobriety and plainness and some thought that leaving the dial corners blank was more true to that principle. Some Quakers engraved verses on their dials about man's transitory state and the approaching day of judgment. Some Quakers used a diamond-shaped half-hour marker rather than a fleur-de-lys, simply because it was more restrained. On the other hand, other Quakers, like Thomas Ogden of Halifax, often did excessively ornate engraving, quite contrary to the Quaker principle. Yet he was reputedly a devout and strict Quaker, even going as far as to address all he met as 'friend' and referring to them in the 'thee and thou' form – a manner of address used by strict Quakers.

All these stylistic features just mentioned, which were used by some Quakers and might be an indication of Quaker work, were also used at other times by non-Quakers, so their presence on a clock dial may not be very helpful in this respect. I've done a lot of research into the group of 'Quaker' clockmakers centred around Wigton, Cumberland, and led by John Sanderson. The more research one does, the more it emerges that the answers are far from simple. Some of the Wigton group were not Quakers, but worked in the Quaker style.

In short we can recognize some Quaker work, but only some, and by no means all unsigned clocks are Quaker-made. Most are mysteriously unsigned for reasons unknown to us. It does not really matter whether a particular clock is Quaker made or not. Quakers, however, were selling in a hostile environment to many who were non-Quakers. They had to give good value for money and developed a reputation for good workmanship and honest trading. This was their method of adhering to principles of honour and forcing their way into a commercial market at the same time. Some Quaker work is excellent in quality, whilst some is crude and primitive. The Oxfordshire Quaker-made hook-and-spike clocks, for instance, are often of very poor quality – interesting but feeble. So identifying a clock as being Quaker work is more a matter of interest than an indication of something special.

8   Reproductions, Copies, Marriages and Fakes

I can think of no type of antique British clock that has not been faked. In addition, there are many clocks, probably the majority, that are not the same today as they were when they were made. These include copies of older styles made either today, or in the past. A modern reproduction clock in a sense is a copy, but not one that is likely to deceive anyone because modern reproduction clocks tend to be designed with mass production and mass markets in mind. They are therefore, to a great extent, made by machines rather than craftsmen, and they are very often made with a mixture of stylistic features of quite widely separate periods that would never appear together on any genuine antique clock. In general they tend to be a real mishmash of styles with the emphasis usually being on smallness to appeal to even the lowest-ceilinged buyer. Nobody is likely, therefore, to think that a modern reproduction clock is old. Even one made fifty years ago would be obviously modern.

One possible exception is the water clock which was made as a novelty in the early years of this century. These were made of brass (or sometimes copper) in a primitive design to hang on the wall. They carried ancient-looking names such as 'Robert Smythe in ye old towne of Bathe', had a single hand which registered the time and was driven by water dripping from a canister. Having been polished for seventy years or so, these now have a glow of age about them, and people who own them stolidly believe that they are very ancient relics from the seventeenth century or before.

I recall once being asked by a neighbour to look at his clock, which was one of these as I explained to him. Clearly he still was inclined to cling to his illusion of its age and some months later he wrote to a monthly antiques magazine to ask their opinion. What he didn't know was that I did their clock queries for them, so again he got the same answer. I had to smile when some months later still he wrote to a clocks magazine, for whom it happened I also did the queries, so he got the same answer for a third time.

To this day he probably thinks that none of us know what we're doing and believes his clock to be a rare 300-year-old gem.

Most water clocks, if not all of them, were made by Pearson, Page & Co. of Birmingham who were still selling them in the 1920s brand new from £3 5s to £8. An advertisement for them appears in *The Connoisseur* of June 1920 with illustrations, so if you have one, you may be able to trace your model there. Genuine antique water clocks do not exist, but even so these crop up in auctions now and then and uninformed buyers can bid wildly for them. Oddly enough modern reproductions of them have been made in more recent times.

Most grandmother and granddaughter clocks are modern. They are copies of older longcase clocks (but smaller in stature) and come readily into the recognizable field of reproductions, even though they now have a few years of age on their backs. They often stand only four or five feet tall and many have spring-driven movements so that they do not need the height of weight-drop which a full size grandfather clock needed. Hence a grandmother clock could be any height for it was essentially a spring-driven mantel clock on a pedestal. Most have German-made movements, recognizable by one of many trademarks on the back of the movement. Most have no name on the dial, but sometimes a British retailer's name appears which is often a furniture shop or department store.

Regular names and marks are Junghans or W&H (Winterhalder & Hoffmeyer) and often a long serial number is present also. If you want to check on the trade mark of a particular one, you will not find it in any book on British clocks, but try a book called *Clock Types*, by E.J. Tyler (Longmans, 1982) which lists many of them.

Some were made with chimes such as Westminster, Whittington or Cambridge, being made specifically for the English market. These chimes did not originate till the late nineteenth century and their presence on a clock is usually an indication that it has no great age. Sometimes such a chime was added later on to what was an older chimeless clock, and this is usually obvious as the extra chime train would be bolted on as an addition. More often an older dial was used to house a late nineteenth-century movement with these chimes.

These clocks usually chime on gongs rather than bells, which chiming English clocks used. They could be coiled wire gongs, straight brass rods or tubular chimes, often depending on the quality of the clock. Any of these three systems indicate that the clock is not British-made, but probably German. Occasionally one sees an antique English longcase which struck the hour on a

Month-duration twelve-inch clock *circa* 1715–20 by Peter King of Long Acre, London. Low winding squares are often an indication of a month movement.

The Peter King clock in its case of fine marquetry of the arabesque type. Height with original caddy about 7 ft. 10 in. Plus points: large amount of marquetry which is even on the hood pillars and the mouldings, and original caddy top.

gong, but in my experience this is always a replacement for a former bell, and examination will reveal where the bell was formerly fixed.

Grandmother or granddaughter clocks are names often used interchangeably to signify the same thing, though some people believe that granddaughters are smaller than grandmothers. They are not antique clocks in the true sense of the word, though some are now almost a hundred years old. Most, however, date from the 1920s and later. Some have finely made mahogany cases, but many, on the other hand, are of cheap quality and made of oak-faced plywood.

Old 'reproduction' clocks were sometimes made (longcases principally, but also lantern clocks) even a hundred years ago or more, copying clocks that were by then already a hundred years old. In particular, these Victorian copies were often scaled-down versions of the grander antique clocks in walnut or mahogany. Some are beautifully made with exquisite workmanship of a far superior quality to most of the 1920 types. It is these miniature late nineteenth-century copies of late eighteenth-century clocks which today pass for 'genuine' antique grandmother clocks, and indeed they are antique themselves now and have a century of patina and finish to them. They are not as old, however, as their style suggests and 'Queen Anne' and 'Georgian' examples are in fact late Victorian copies. Even if you are willing to believe that 'Queen Anne' clocks were still being made in 1770 there are ways of proving that these clocks are 'wrong'.

If the cases have acquired a genuine age to them by now (100 years passing for 200 or 300), the clocks they house can be easily identified as being 'made up'. The tiny dials might be approximately six inches wide and there simply were no longcase dials of that size. The copyists probably used complete hooded wall clocks with their original thirty-hour movements or else added an eight-day movement from some other (full size) longcase to the tiny dial of a hooded clock. This latter process would normally involve drilling winding-holes through the chapter ring. The absence of seconds dials on such clocks indicates that these dials were originally thirty-hour dials (which didn't have this feature).

Almost all genuine eight-day clocks (and longer durations) do have a seconds dial, except in cases where some other feature might occupy the space below XII. So any eight-day clock without a seconds dial needs close inspection for possible alterations. Grandmother clocks don't (usually) have seconds dials because miniature seconds rings were not available as standard items. Sometimes a clockmaker would make one specially for a grandmother clock he was working on, and those are usually distinctly different in engraving nature and style from the main chapter ring, since engraving of 1900 is very different from engraving of 1770.

A grandmother clock could have been made with a dial from a bracket clock, but bracket clocks were too costly to break up for this purpose, whilst thirty-hour hooded clocks were not. A bracket clock dial already had two winding-holes drilled in it, but they would mostly have been wrongly positioned for a longcase movement. A hooded dial could have had a matted centre in which type two winding-holes could be drilled without breaking any centre pattern. On the type with an engraved centre, the newly drilled holes would cut into the pattern, and winding holes which break the dial centre pattern are suspicious on any clock.

Even with a matted centre type the winding-holes for use on a normal eight-day longcase movement might be too widely spaced for a tiny hooded dial, perhaps even cutting into the chapter ring. Most grandmother clocks would use a normal (scrap) longcase movement which were (and still are) very cheaply available.

Most hooded clocks do not have box calendars. Those which do have any calendar at all are in the minority and then they tend to have the mouth type calendar which needs only a pin to drive it, rather than an extra wheel which the box type needs. So grandmother clocks normally have no calendar, or if they do have no mechanism to drive it, unless by luck the hour pipe ran close enough and a pin could quite easily be fitted. A glance behind the dial will usually show that the movement (like most eight-day longcase ones) has a seconds arbor protrusion to carry a seconds hand, though it may have been cut off short to camouflage that fact. It may also then be seen that the movement has a hole where once a twenty-four hour calendar drive wheel fitted. Therefore a movement carrying a seconds feature and perhaps also a calendar feature – neither of which appear in the dial – is a dead giveaway. If a falseplate has been used, this is a further giveaway. If not, there are almost certainly spare holes in the movement frontplate indicating that a different dial once belonged to it.

Of course, a clever maker of grandmother clocks may have filled up empty holes in the frontplate to disguise his alteration. These are well camouflaged when brightly polished, but usually tarnish at a different rate to the plate itself, so that with the passing of a few years the filled holes show easily. An even more careful maker could have made brand new plates and re-laid the two trains of wheels to bring them closer together so that the winding-holes were not unduly wide apart. They seldom took this amount of trouble however.

The maker of grandmother clocks also had trouble with spandrels as there were no tiny ones to fit this size of dial, unless, of course, the hooded dial already had them (as some did) or he used reproduction ones. If he used repro ones of the day (1900) or even original ones, then just about the only pattern small enough to fit would be the tiny winged cherub-head type as found on the very oldest London clocks of the 1680s. On a grandmother clock purporting to be of the 1780s these would be incongruous to say the least.

Sometimes the maker of grandmother clocks would make his own new dial sheet to get around the problem of winding-holes cutting through an engraved design. If he did he would use new brass of the day, which was rolled brass of uniform thickness, whereas a 1790 brass dial was made out of cast brass of uneven thickness and usually much hammered and filed during cleaning before use. Cast brass also tends to have numerous tiny imperfections such as small blow holes, whilst rolled brass is more perfect. The beginner may have difficulty knowing rolled brass from cast at first, but after examining a few genuine brass-dial clocks from the eighteenth century, nineteenth-century rolled brass will look different. Both are equally subject to tarnishing so don't be taken in by a dirty surface, corrosion, or imitated corrosion which has been painted on.

By and large the maker of grandmother clocks was making use of waste movements and parts and did not want to go to great lengths or great expense to conceal any alterations. Most were not made as 'fakes' but just as a way of satisfying demand whilst using up scrap parts. Seldom would a nameplate be made specially and he might often use a full size nameplate from an old longcase dial which would therefore be oversize. A hooded clock nameplate would obviously be the right size. Names were seldom engraved on to the work specially as this meant more expense, but if they are the style of engraving will be much different from older engraving.

A dial made without using a hooded dial was a problem in so far as there were no tiny chapter rings, except perhaps those from an old lantern clock which were single-handed chapter rings. If he used one of these he would normally mark minutes all the way around by using a drill. A lantern clock ring is instantly recognizable once you have seen one and these did not indicate minutes.

Cases for 'antique' grandmother clocks may be beautifully made, though most were not. Many were simple cottage thirty-hour cases cut down in size. Thus all, or nearly all, exterior surfaces are genuinely old. Some are very well made

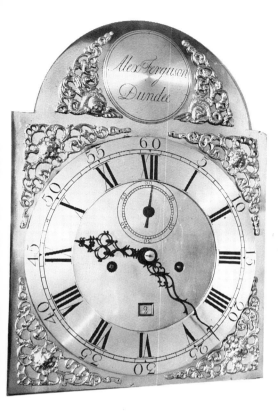

Twelve-inch dial of eight-day clock of about
1780 by Alexander Ferguson of Dundee.
Absence of half-hour or inner chapter-ring
markings typical of this later period. Plain
polished dial centre.

All-mahogany case of the clock by Ferguson of
Dundee, *circa* 1780. The mahogany is solid with
limited figuring mainly on the door and base.
Very clean condition, pale colour with hood
side windows which are common to many
Scottish cases. Value points on this clock are its
clean condition and exceptionally small size
(only 6 ft. 7 in).

'Chippendale' style cases in miniature or 'Queen Anne' style versions in walnut. These by now have a good colour and surface patina. When you come to examine details in the style of them, there are usually inconsistencies and incongruities about them, in terms of features of the casework. For instance, you might find a 'Queen Anne' period clock with 1770 dial style features. Each grandmother clock will have to be taken as a one-off, which they were, and compared with stylistic details of full size clocks (supposedly) of the same period, these inconsistencies will usually be plainly visible.

Sometimes grandmother clocks were (and still are) made by cutting down large unsaleable clocks such as the big Victorian 'Yorkshire' clocks as they are sometimes called. Such clocks are taken apart, reduced in size, re-assembled, fitted up with a cut down painted dial and eight-day movement. All visible external surfaces, therefore, are truly old. Any inner alterations can be disguised with a coat of cabinetmaker's special gunge that makes a new piece of timber look 200 years old as soon as it dries. Ten years ago a £150 'Yorkshire' clock could be re-made into a £1,500 grandmother clock in just this way. Today such a clock might cost £500 and could be turned into a £2,500 grandmother – so there's still profit in it even allowing for all the alteration work.

The inherent problems in making grandmother clocks also applied in making 'marriages'. Suppose a painted dial were removed from a clock movement and a brass dial substituted. First of all, the four (sometimes three) dial feet would not fit into the existing holes in the new movement frontplate. As a result the faker had to fill the holes and drill new ones, or leave the holes empty, which he normally did. He could alternatively move the position of the dial feet so they fitted. Another possibility was to use a falseplate to help the fitting process as falseplates were never originally used with brass dials.

This kind of alteration will usually be very easy to see. A falseplate will also often have a dialmaker's name on it which is almost certain to clash with the period of the name on any brass dial. Incidentally, all the names can be checked in *Watchmakers and Clockmakers of the World*. In any case, however, *any* brass dial clock with a falseplate is an alteration, so there is no need to check dates as it is quite simply wrong.

Replacing a painted dial with a brass one may have involved using an existing brass dial discarded from some other clock. In this case not only will the fitting of the dial feet be a problem, but the four holes in the dial (two winding-squares, one seconds hole, one hands hole, and possibly a fifth hole for the calendar) will need to line up with these same four functions in the movement, or will need some shuffling about. A calendar feature and seconds feature are often blanked off in these cases because of a bad fit. If an old thirty-hour dial was used, the faker could drill his winding-holes where he wanted them, but the absence of a seconds dial is a giveaway, especially if a glance inside shows that the movement has seconds drive which is not being used.

Sometimes the man who replaced a painted dial with a brass one would make a brand new dial. If so the rolled brass will be a giveaway and so will the engraving style and quality.

Beware of the brass dial with its back painted over in black paint or black gunge, as this is sometimes done to conceal lack of age or filled holes, or both. I remember a dealer trying to sell me one once where the black paint was still wet and came off in my hands while holding the movement! I came across the clock again some year or two later in the home of a 'collector', but the paint had had time to dry by then.

Brass dials were often fitted to longcases to replace worn or jaded painted dials, especially early in this century when brass dials were thought worthwhile and painted dials less so. I don't think anyone has yet taken to removing brass dials to replace with painted ones, as the price imbalance is the wrong way and someone trying this would soon go bankrupt.

What does happen today, however, is that spare dials and movements without dials often turn up in auction and the wily often buy these to build up a collection of permutations which they can make up into 'complete' clocks. Such parts go quite cheaply at auction. We all know the type of dealers who buy them. If such a movement cost say £100 and such a dial say £50, then for £150 one clock can be made out of the two, when a genuine clock (dial and movement complete) might ordinarily cost several hundred pounds. This is where the problem of justifying buying a 'marriage' falls down because many marriages were made recently by people who buy loose parts to re-sell as complete clocks. So the buyer who knowingly and willingly buys a marriage is exactly the person such 'marriages' were made up for, and perhaps only a few months before.

Eight-day clocks have always been more popular in recent times than thirty-hour ones, so clock bodgers have often been enterprising enough to make thirty-hour clocks into eight-day ones. This was done by replacing the thirty-hour movement with an eight-day one, usually from a painted dial clock of little value or perhaps using a loose movement bought at auction as scrap. A thirty-hour would normally have no seconds dial, and the absence of such makes one look more carefully at an eight-day, since most eight-days had them. Two winding-holes need to be cut into the dial and this often meant cutting into the engraving or perhaps the calendar work. Converting a thirty-hour into an eight-day involves most of the problems outlined earlier in grandmother clockmaking and the signs are almost always there if you care to look for them.

So marriages of dial and movement are almost always easy to spot. If a faker had gone to a great deal of trouble, as he might with a clock bearing a famous name, then he would disguise most of these changes and they would not be easily found. Seldom is such degree of trouble taken with ordinary clocks however.

Not all marriages are modern. Some were done a hundred years ago. If a clock movement was very worn, it was thought a better proposition to replace it with one in good order. Therefore it may not have been done with the intention of deceiving then, but may now deceive all the same. Some believe that age justifies an old alteration, from which I deduce that those who would object to being deceived by the living, don't object to being deceived by those long dead. In any case, who can tell the age of an alteration? Not many, which is why those who do it today manage to thrive.

So marriages of movement and dial are not too hard to spot in longcase clocks. Bracket clocks are more difficult, but oddly enough much less subject to it. Lantern clocks are often made up, but that sort of job is beyond the ability of a novice to recognize until he gains some experience. The same problems apply to nearly all of these if married, that is the faker had to try to camouflage his alterations. Empty or filled holes are always a giveaway.

Another kind of marriage is where the movement with dial are genuine and belong together, but the case is not the one the clock started out with. The reasons for changing clockcases are numerous. Changes occurred because of bad condition, woodworm, a taste for a newer style, a move to a house with smaller ceilings, or even just a whim of the second-hand buyer. It was quite common in recent years for a dealer to offer to swap a case for you if you so desired. It probably still happens today.

If you wish you can justify a marriage of case to movement by pointing out that, when it was first made, the clock was in any event a marriage of the work of two quite different craftsmen, i.e. the clockmaker and the casemaker. This is of course true. All the same that clock was originally in the case it was first sold with, and remains original only as long as the two stay together. Furthermore it would be a case made in a certain region at a certain date, and the great likelihood is that a replacement case may not only have been made at a completely different period,

A good eight-day clock by Thomas Armstrong of Hawkshead made about 1790 with thirteen-inch Wilson dial. Plus features: rolling moon, original hands throughout, well-restored dial, flower-corners, movement numbered (no.33), unusually late use of the word 'fecit'.

but in a different area where styles were nothing like those of the original. If the case *was* of the right period and the right style, then it might be argued that the marriage was of no great detriment to the clock (though the original case must obviously have been far better from all points of view). Who is to say, however, that the replacement case *is* of the same period or area? I doubt if a handful of people in the land have that sort of knowledge, yet almost anyone trying to sell such a marriage would claim he did and that the replacement case was contemporary and compatible.

Most swapped cases are later than the clock they now house. This is because cases deteriorate quicker than clocks. If you like a particular clock you may well accept that it will suit you, even though you may know the case is non-original. This is a decision only you can make, as the buyer.

What is important, however, is that you make your decision *knowing* whether the case is original to the clock or not. In the majority of instances it is quite easy to recognize one from the other. Most swapped cases can be readily identified as such, so can the majority of cases which are right to the movement. In the no man's land in between is a small area where it is difficult to be certain. This is where, if a change has taken place, the style is so simple that it gives little clue as to period or region. Where, by chance, seatboard arrangements fail to offer the usual vital clues, or where a faker has very carefully concealed the usual telltale signs of change it is also very difficult to be sure about the case. So, in establishing whether the case is original what points do you look for?

A longcase clock movement sits on a wooden shelf called a seatboard. Eight-day clocks are usually bolted to the seatboard, either with bolts that fit into the lower movement pillars or else with seatboard hooks which fit over them. Thirty-hour clocks sometimes sit loose on their fixed boards, but purely for convenience in handling the modern practice is to bolt these to their boards too. Any clock is easier to move if it is fastened to its seatboard in this way. The seatboard normally sits on two upright 'cheeks' with one at each side of the case. Sometimes the seatboard is nailed to the cheeks for safety. Often this was done when the clock was first made, and if the seatboard remains tightly nailed down then a repairer has to untie the gutline ends and thread the lines out to remove the clock. This is a fiddly business and awkward for those not used to it. It is much more convenient to remove any nails and take out movement with seatboard for any cleaning or repairing.

Therefore, whether or not the board was originally nailed down, today most are not. Even an unnailed seatboard usually has at some time in its life been secured, perhaps by some cautious owner. Some clocks are front-heavy and, if the seatboard is narrow, may be inclined to tilt forward ominously when assembling. So, for safety, many have had a variety of nails or screws to hold the boards tight to the cheeks. The first test then for originality of case is to see whether any holes in the seatboard line up with holes in the cheeks, whether nails still are in place or not. Holes in one which do not line up with holes in the other are bad news and indicate a changed seatboard. Obviously one must take into account possible mis-positioning of the board where some owner may have fitted it too far forward or too far back at some time in its life. If the seatboard is original to the movement then wrongly aligned holes indicate a change of case.

A replacement seatboard could be a valid reason why such holes do not line up. It is, of course, a very convenient trick for someone marrying two items together, as the new seatboard removes the evidence which would otherwise be visible. A new seatboard therefore (or even an old one not original to the movement, *if* you can detect this) is a warning light to most buyers, because there is seldom a valid reason for replacing a seatboard. One which was badly wormed, split, warped or sagging from strain could have been changed for that reason, but these are infrequent occurrences. If I replace a seatboard myself, I usually keep the old one so that the buyer can see the reason for its being replaced. Few owners are likely to keep a wormy seatboard as evidence for long, and with one change of ownership, such evidence usually goes on the bonfire. So a new seatboard may only be a warning sign and not damning evidence, but it is something to take into account with other clues.

Another way of camouflaging the non-alignment of holes is to leave the original seatboard and replace the cheeks. So replaced cheeks are a warning sign. On many cases the cheeks are a continuation of the case sides, which were left overlength when the clock was made and were cut to the right size according to the clock's fitting position. Replaced cheeks are often joined behind the moulding so that the joints don't show and this is the place to check.

Sometimes a packing piece is inserted between the cheeks and the seatboard to correct the height position of the dial/movement when put into a different case. Packing spacers could be tiny (less than a quarter of an inch) or quite large (an inch or two), but their presence again is a warning sign. There can be quite valid reasons for packing pieces, but if I set these out, that will give every case-swapper the excuses he is looking for, so I don't propose doing that. Packing pieces are normally quite obviously newer than other timbers they attach to. Fakers often stain them to make them look old and less conspicuous.

The dial of most clocks sits in its case behind a mask or inner frame inside the hood door. The mask usually overlaps the dial at its edge all round by maybe a quarter of an inch or a bit less. This is set back from the glass (and hood door) by maybe an inch. So with, for instance, a twelve-inch square dial, the hood door (glass) size may be twelve inches, but the mask might be eleven and a half or eleven and three-quarters. The visible fit becomes correct by virtue of the distance back from the glass of the mask suiting the angle of vision. Anyone who puts a twelve-inch dial into an eleven-inch case has a problem in that part of the dial features would be obscured. He may therefore open up the mask aperture to let the full dial show. Therefore, a mask where the corner joints are cut into is a sign that the case has been altered to allow the present dial to 'fit'. The hood door itself is less often altered as that would have been a more difficult job and more obviously visible.

An altered mask shows its alteration at the joints, and possibly also by its newer, re-cut edges – though these are sometimes dulled down with stain for camouflage. Sometimes a case-swapper thought it easier or less obvious if he replaced the mask completely with a new one and he might stain it to conceal its newness. A mask was rarely stained originally, but usually left in the raw oak or more commonly pine. So the staining of a mask can itself be a warning sign. Sometimes, if a smaller dial is fitted to a larger case, the mask may have a beaded edge mould added to reduce its opening all round. I find it hard to think of a genuine reason for an altered mask on a case which is original to the clock. I did once sell a clock to a dealer who was new to the business and that clock had a mask which was very close to the dial, so close in fact that he later thought it was the wrong case for the clock, so he set about cutting and sanding away the edges of the mask to make it fit 'better'. Having done that, of course, he had unwittingly produced a situation where the clock really did look as if it was in the wrong case.

An eight-day case and a thirty-hour case are not quite the same thing. For instance, an eight-day case will normally have been fitted with a door lock and a thirty-hour will not. Would you want to unlock and lock the door every day? There are exceptions but by and large a thirty-hour case will have a turnbuckle knob and an eight-day will have a lock or there will be signs of where they had originally been, because many cases no longer have their original fastening work. A thirty-hour case will usually be a simpler and less costly affair than an eight-day. Moreover the

Thirteen-inch white-dial clock with moonwork
by Cawson of Lancaster, *circa* 1790. Note
double Arabic numbering (minutes and hours).
The all-mahogany case stands 7 ft. 7 in. The
case shows several Gillow features such as the
semi-circular door top and the kink within the
circle of the swan necks. Plus points: condition,
restrained styling, modest height,
attributable case, slender bamboo-simulated
pillars, moonwork.

weight rubs will show in different areas on each type. A thirty-hour has a single weight, which sometimes rubs as the clock runs. Two centuries of rubbing weight may well have worn a *single* groove inside the upper door framework below the hood and another one below the trunk door. Depending on the narrowness of the case and the fit of the clock the rub may show in only one of these two places rather than in both. A thirty-hour will have a single rub mark, which is usually easily felt with the hand. This is most often found somewhere in the centre of the case.

An eight-day clock will have two rub marks, one from each of its two weights and these will be positioned equally across the case front – roughly either side of where the central thirty-hour rubbing-point would be. Weight rubs may also show on the inside of the trunk door. So, quite simply, a case which may seem to you to have a thirty hour look about it (and one soon develops the knack of judging this) and has a single weight rub, is clearly wrong if it has an eight-day clock in it. Likewise a double weight rub case could not originally have housed a thirty-hour clock. Case-swappers know this of course, and may well plane away any tell tale rub marks, then cover the new rubbings with stain to make them less obvious. This is why you need your inspection torch to look inside a longcase at parts you cannot easily see in its assembled state.

The pendulum bob on most longcases will at some time or other have caught against and scuffed the backboard, for example when the case may have been leaning too far backwards. Such a pendulum rub mark is caused either by the back of the rounded bob, which leaves a soft rubbing or bruising mark, or else by the sharper edge of the rating nut which is more likely to score a scratch. If the pendulum on the clock which is presently in that case does not rub against the backboard in those positions, it is more than likely that another clock was previously housed in that case. Of course the pendulum may not be the original one, as these do sometimes get lost in auction, mixed up or renewed from rust and so on. A new pendulum, however, would have to be of the same length as the old one, or the clock would not keep time. A larger or smaller bob than before might just affect the rub point slightly, but not by any considerable distance such as an inch or more. If you buy a clock in dismantled state, such as in auction, you cannot see where the pendulum rubs. The answer is to hang it on, or if the suspension spring has broken, then hold it in place so that you can judge the rub points *before* you bid.

Alterations to the inside wooden fittings in longcases were often stained to disguise them. But stain dribbles into unintended places, so search for signs of stain runs. The original cabinetmaker was selling a brand new piece of furniture, so he had no need to stain anything inside a case. Inside stain is a suspicious sign. Sometimes one sees a backboard stained (or even painted) all over, and this may well have been to remove traces of old rub marks that no longer line up with present day features. Sometimes cases with pine structures inside, particularly Victorian ones, have a coat of red lead paint as an aid against woodworm. On such examples the pendulum scratch would have scored through the paint layer and should still be visible.

Sometimes in a narrow case the pendulum might swing so far side to side as to tap on the side of the case. This might be a sign that the clock is in the wrong case. Even if, as sometimes happens, a hole has later been cut in the case side to allow a tap-free swing, it might still be the original case. What happens when a clock is overhauled is that the escapement pallets are often renewed or re-shaped to account for wear and in doing so most restorers like to give the clock a good 'healthy' swing. So healthy the restored swing can be sometimes, that the pendulum may tap, and owners unaware of the correct solution may cut holes or tack foam pads inside to quieten a tapping clock. Such tapping may in any event play havoc with the time-keeping, as the swing will build up pace slowly, then tap, thus reducing its swing and then build up again. So a tapping clock is often inconsistent in its tapping and time-keeping and an absolute irritation to live with.

A clock in the wrong case will often be obvious at a distance of thirty paces – so obvious in fact that one need not even look inside for some of the signs of alteration just mentioned. Familiarity with case styles can be acquired to some degree from studying cases in books. Certain regions have very strong stylistic trends which are unique to those regions. A London case of whatever period is usually quite distinctive in style; it will be different from a provincial clock of the same period. Strong regional trends pertain to other areas too, such as Bristol and the West Country, Lancashire, the Lakes, the North East (Tyneside), East Yorkshire, Lincolnshire, East Anglia, Birmingham and the Midlands – these are some of the obvious ones. If you see a clock from Norwich in a Bristol case, it can't possibly be right. But before you can recognize this, you must be able to distinguish one from the other and a novice will not have that expertise.

The ability to recognize the period of a case is something which the novice may also lack, though this is not so hard to acquire as a knowledge of regional styles, especially if he has some knowledge of antique furniture. Almost all clockmakers can be dated by checking their names in *Watch and Clockmakers of the World* (two volumes). Does the period when the clockmaker is known to have worked tally with the apparent age of the case? If you are not sure, then ask the vendor, and also ask him how he can recognize the period of the case. Most who know will be delighted to tell you.

If one or perhaps even two of the points discussed suggest that the case is not original to the clock, this is not necessarily proof. There can be reasons why most of these features might happen and yet still be on a clock which is original to its case. Where several features fail to tally, however then you have absolute proof. The tell tale signs almost always involve alterations to make a clock fit into a case it was never intended to fit into. Almost always the signs are there if you look for them, but you also need to look out for such signs that the case-swapper has tried to camouflage.

I ought to mention the question of carved cases in this section. These are not really fakes or forgeries, but most are in fact alterations achieved by carving the surface of an older clock at a much later date thereby changing it totally. There are probably some carved cases which were carved when they were first made. Most, however, were once eighteenth-century oak cases carved about 1900 with decorative designs or patterns. The carving is often limited to the front of the clock, but sometimes the sides are carved too. Many were stained after carving to a very dark brown colour with a thick stain (almost like a paint) which obscures the grain.

Some people like carved clocks and why not? Those who want a carved case should know, however, that the carving is almost always much later – a hundred years or more later – than the clock itself. I've often heard claims that a particular carved clock was carved at the time of making, but never yet have I seen proof of this. Proof that a clock was carved later is often much easier to come by from an examination of the clock. It is sufficient here, however, to say that almost all were carved later.

Many carved cases have mahogany crossbanding on to an oak body. The carving often cuts in on the mahogany, which in any case is usually almost obscured by the black stain. Both of these features are signs that the case was never meant to be carved. Many a good clock has been spoiled and once carved it is difficult to 'un-carve' it, though oddly I did come across an example not long ago.

A dealer offered me a clock by a highly reputed maker, but although the clock was in its original case the case door had been carved later. The carving was only to the door, but nevertheless it put me off it completely. Some time later I called round on that dealer again and saw another clock by this same reputable maker. It looked vaguely familiar, but I couldn't place it, which in itself was odd because dealers don't usually forget. Remembering what you've seen before, and where and how much it was are things which are an integral part of the business. It was maybe a year later, however, and I had completely forgotten about the clock with the carved door by now. Eventually the dealer explained that it was the same clock. What he had done was to have the door removed, plane it down far enough to remove the carving and laminate another piece of oak to the door front – thick enough to bring the overall thickness to that which it formerly had. The new surface was stained and coloured to a very good match, and it looked no more than an example of a re-polished door. Everything on the inside was clearly original. Now this is not recognized practice, but probably only because few have thought of it before. Whether you regard this as acceptable treatment or not, it was certainly one way of getting over the problem of later carving.

9 Where to Buy and How

There is a favourite quotation of mine from an advertisement of 1807 placed by clockmaker John Begg of Edinburgh, which proves that nothing's changed:

> Trade was driven into the hands of those who were not trained, so that there is scarcely a cloth shop or hardware shop that does not deal in watches, who know no more about a watch than a cow does of a new-coined shilling.

In Britain there are perhaps a score of dealers who make a living buying and selling antique clocks. I am one myself. They are professionals in every sense of the word. They have put time, effort and every penny they own, or can borrow, into the business of studying, buying and understanding antique clocks. Some have devoted most of their lives to it. Of the many thousands of antique clocks appearing on the market each year, these professionals choose the ones they want to buy, put their money into them, usually research the makers and the unusual or interesting aspects of each clock, put them into full working order and offer them for sale.

Their accumulated knowledge is formidable and at the disposal of any customer free of charge. They will discuss your needs with you and advise you to the best of their abilities, hoping obviously to sell you a clock. Imagine, if you can, discussing a problem with a solicitor or accountant for an hour or two and then departing to consider whether or not you will do business with him; you certainly would not get that advice free of charge. So if you know there are specialist clock dealers and you decide to ignore them in your search for a clock, you are immediately depriving yourself of the nation's largest bank of knowledge on the subject.

These specialist dealers cover *every* auction and between them they miss nothing. If they don't buy it, it's not because they don't know about it, but because they don't want it. Either something is wrong with it (commercially speaking) or it is too expensive. If you think as a private individual short on experience and knowledge that you can beat the experts at their own game, you are deluding yourself. Now I know as I write this that there are those who think that they know better. They think they know a little auction in a remote mountain village where bargains slip by unnoticed, a little old lady a few doors away whose heirloom they can take off her hands for a few quid or a 'private collector' who won't sell to dealers. What they don't know is that the specialists cover the remote mountain-top auction room every Friday, that the little old lady's clock is a wrong-un and they turned it down three weeks ago, and that the 'private collector' is a dealer himself pretending not to be, in the hope that the tax man will fail to spot his activities.

People may imagine that a specialist dealer's clock will be more expensive than a similar clock 'picked up' elsewhere. Generally speaking this is not so. Certainly you will not be able to buy a £10,000 clock from a specialist for £2,000, but neither can you buy one anywhere else in the land for that price. You will have to pay the going rate. Remember the specialist has to face every other specialist and knowledgeable collector and, by and large, his prices must reflect reality. On the other hand, other sources may vastly overprice their clocks, even if simply from the uninformed standpoint that as they see few of them then they must be very rare things indeed.

A specialist dealer must know what he is selling. He is obliged to know whether the clock is genuine and what alterations, if any, have been done to it. Virtually all specialists will give a guarantee that it works properly. Those who sell the occasional clock can pretend (genuinely or otherwise) that they don't know much about clocks and it seems all right as far as they can tell. An outspoken customer might venture to ask why, if they don't know much about clocks, they have the audacity to sell them. So if you choose to buy a clock from a dealer who openly admits to knowing little about what he is selling, you can hardly grumble if the clock you end up with proves to be not all you first thought it to be.

The sources where you might buy an antique clock are basically: a specialist clock dealer, a general antique dealer, a junk shop, an antique fair, an auction or the old lady next door. Not all of these sources are as straightforward as you might first think, and it might help to understand some of the less obvious aspects of some of these.

All kinds of events pass under the name of 'antique fair' these days, from pompous affairs in gilded halls where you are afraid to turn over a price ticket for fear of a heart attack to village jumble sales offering 1950s junk. Most fairs are somewhere in the middle and are the kind of thing I've heard described unkindly as 'the usual travelling circus', meaning a regular event where a number of dealers gather goods together for sale in a particular venue once or twice a year. The idea, of course, is that the public of the locality has the opportunity of seeing a large number of items for sale under one roof. It was a great idea twenty years ago when fairs were relatively new, but the vast proliferation of fairs today has caused confusion in the public mind. When there may be as many as half a dozen different fairs in the same town each year and often one-day events every weekend, the public has difficulty remembering which were the ones with high standards and which were the junky ones. Fair organizers therefore try hard to make their own imprint on the public mind. Many also try to set minimum standards and have 'vetting committees' whose job is to ensure that inferior items are not on offer – that is items younger than the specified age or over-restored and fake items.

At any of the better antique fairs there are usually quite a number of clocks on sale, and from the buyer's point of view the bigger the selection, the better. There are highly reputable dealers who display at fairs and there are others who do not exist at all outside the three- or four-day life of that fair. I've seen antique fairs where the name above a particular stand has been coined for the particular occasion. So if you buy at an antique fair, check first that the vendors do have some permanent establishment somewhere. Otherwise, if you have a problem with your purchase, you have nowhere to turn to for satisfaction later.

One aspect which novices seem quite unaware of, is that the standholder has to pay a fee for his stand and in some fairs that can run to thousands of pounds. He also has to pay carriage for his goods, transit insurance, hotel bills for himself and staff for a week or more, and close down his home business or employ extra staff there during his absence. It seems to me only common sense that those extra costs must go on to the price of his goods somehow, unless they are already priced high enough to absorb those extras. The bonus for the dealer of course is that a busy antique fair may see a large through-put of spenders. When I see a dealer from the south of England displaying in a fair in the north of Scotland, however, it seems to me that it tells one a great deal about the state of business back home, but that may just be my cynical view.

Those who imagine they will run into a bargain at an antique fair will want to dash in through the turntable bang on opening time before the goods get picked up. That is what some dealers like to do and some fairs may even let the trade in before the general public, as the trade are likely to be big spenders. Some dealers, perhaps the more astute, will visit the fair on the last hour of the last day when the standholders are faced with the imminent prospect of packing everything up again and hauling it several hundred miles back home. Whether the fair has been a successful one or not, it is surprising how prices can tumble at that moment and offers may be accepted then which would have been derided three days earlier.

The whole question of whether or not to make an offer for an item is a tricky one. Some dealers price goods way up in order to be able to drop an amazing degree and the naïve are taken in by this. I was once looking at a bookcase in an antiques shop with a tag indicating that the price was £3,000. The dealer, who was a total stranger to me approached me and said I should ignore the price tag and I could have it for £2,000. My reaction was one of horror at how disastrous it would have been if I had walked in and bought it for £3,000. On another occasion, I was in a shop when a customer entered to ask the price of a bronze figure in the window which proved to be £1,000. He expressed dismay as his budget limit was £600 and he ventured to say that he didn't suppose the dealer would take £600. 'Yes,' said the dealer, getting out his invoice book and starting to write, 'What name is it?' With characters like this about, it is small wonder the public may be confused.

Most dealers price their goods at a level they know they will sell at. They are professionals and the antiques business is not some sort of game to them. They know exactly what they are doing and how much an item will sell for or fail to sell for. You try making an offer and you are only likely to embarrass yourself and everyone else too, just as you would if you tried the same thing in the grocer's shop or a solicitor's office.

Yet, some people will think that they have heard about such a thing as a 'trade price' which is when a dealer might sell to another dealer at a lower figure than ticketed. So there must be a lower price level to negotiate? Well, yes, because most dealers will offer a trade discount to a trade buyer as a trade buyer buys quickly, repeatedly, without warranty and probably several items at once. A trade buyer will buy a clock in five or ten minutes at most. A private buyer can dither for three hours before finally taking the plunge, if then. If you think, however, you can buy under trade conditions, and are happy to take your clock away with no warranty and no comebacks, then try asking whether the vendor will sell to you at trade terms. If you want to buy several clocks at once, he probably will.

Value Added Tax is chargeable on antiques under current law, and there are two methods by which this may be applied by dealers. The most obvious is to price an item at, for example,

£2,000 plus VAT = £2,350. Some dealers do this because they can't be bothered to operate the much more time-consuming system offered by Customs & Excise as an alternative, which is known as the Antiques Special Scheme and applies only to articles over 100 years old. Most dealers operate this system, as it keeps the price to the customer lower. It involves the dealer paying VAT on his profit margin on each item. That margin is determined for this purpose as being the difference between his buying and selling price, regardless of any restoration or other costs on that item.

Under the Special Scheme if a dealer buys a clock at £200 and sells it at £250 his profit is assumed to be £50, and under the present 17½% VAT rate he pays VAT of 7/47ths of £50 = £7.44. Even if he spent £20 restoring it, that restoration cost is not counted into his 'cost' figure. A buyer who buys an item under the Special Scheme cannot reclaim any VAT.

This system may be confusing to a buyer who has not come across it before and asks the question: does the price include VAT? The answer is that it does (under this system) but that he cannot reclaim any VAT on his purchase and the VAT proportion is only a tiny amount of the total figure he has to pay. As dealers' profit margins are so tiny, he should lose no sleep about it.

Overseas buyers may wonder about the question of whether or not import duty is payable on a clock bought in Britain. The answer is that no duty is payable on items over 100 years old to English speaking countries such as USA, Australia, New Zealand, Canada – provided documentation, such as the invoice, clearly specifies the age of the item and proof of shipment is provided. Australian Customs are notoriously strict about this and will not accept the invoice as being adequate proof of age, as they do not regard the vendor as an impartial agent. They insist on a certification of age by an established authority, such as one of the several Antique Dealers' Associations (BADA, LAPADA, etc) who would need to inspect the item and will charge a fee for this, which can be a bit awkward if it has been crated up and is already *en voyage*. So an overseas buyer should check this aspect carefully with the vendor at the time of purchase.

Antique clocks going into European countries from Britain are charged with import duty based on the current VAT rate of the importing country, regardless of the age of the object. In theory VAT will not have been charged here, but will be charged there instead. Those selling under the Special Scheme, however, may well refuse to deduct the VAT portion, as they are not charging VAT in the normal sense. Selling for export without VAT is complicated and prone to problems, all of which penalize the vendor. A dealer who has exported a clock free of VAT and later

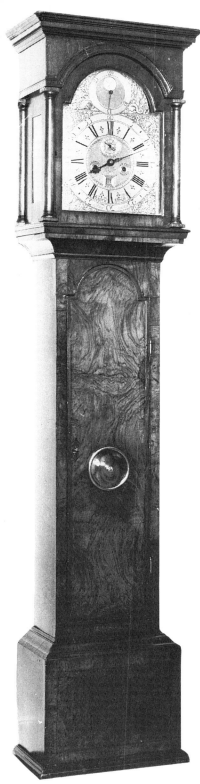

Twelve-inch eight-day clock by Gabriel Smith
of Nantwich, *circa* 1720. Plus points: strong
character in dial, penny moonwork, reputable
maker.

Walnut veneered case (on to oak) of the clock
by Gabriel Smith of Nantwich. Plus points:
lenticle (unusual in arched dial work),
bookmatched veneering, modest height (about
7 ft. 3 in.), reputable maker.

has been made to pay VAT (which he never received) to the Customs & Excise, because he lacked the correct documentation, may not surprisingly feel peeved about it and may throw up his hands in horror at the whole export procedure and thereafter sell only on the Special Scheme whether to home or export buyers. I wouldn't blame him for doing this.

One place you can buy an antique clock is at auction, and this is a method of buying which may have particular appeal to a beginner, who may be excited at the thought of bidding in his own right. Anyone with a bad cough would be unwise to attend auctions, where it can cost as much as £400 per cough! Auctions are, of course, where the dealers buy many of their clocks, so the private buyer can compete there against the trade and buy a clock at a 'trade' price. That is how a beginner may think in his naîvety and every auctioneer in the country will bless him for his innocence.

Auctions always remind me of television. What we see on the screen is entertainment, and not to be confused with reality. The viewer sees what the producer wants him to see and receives the message he wants him to receive. Auctions are not dissimilar.

There are over four hundred auction rooms in Britain. Most hold a sale once a week or once a month. They range from decaying piles of junk in village halls to regal displays of noble furniture in grand city centre 'rooms', where access is a nightmare, and a parking ticket or a clamp are an integral part of the buyer's expenses, though not tax deductible. Most antique auctions will contain a clock or two, so that in any week in Britain many hundreds, even thousands, of antique clocks are offered for sale. Many auction houses today are owned by the large estate agents or building societies, though there are still some independent local auctions. Some have highly experienced and highly qualified staff while others have part-time labour with neither qualifications nor experience. Anyone can open an auction room by hiring a village hall or a marquee and a couple of porters. You could do it yourself next week if you had a mind to, as long as you could round up enough items to offer for sale. You could if you so wished raise enough lots by putting in unwanted items from your own home, or from friends or neighbours. It might be a poor auction and you might not sell your goods, but that's a chance every auctioneer takes, and as that chance is taken with other people's goods, it does not come high in terms of risk taking with venture capital.

So these are the two extremes: the internationally renowned auction houses and the small local auction, which could be run by a schoolteacher on his day off or a nightclub bouncer. No qualifications or experience are required to set up as an auctioneer, though some of course do have both. I point this out simply because the innocent may assume that an auctioneer is in some way an expert in assessing the value of the thing he sells, when he may know no more about it than the man who delivers your milk.

There is nothing to stop an auctioneer offering his own goods for sale in his 'auction', and some do, as there is no requirement in this country for the auctioneer to declare an interest he might have in any item offered for sale. In some countries such an interest has to be declared, and it will probably apply here one day, but for now there are no restrictions. Therefore, in effect, some auctioneers may be dealers in disguise who are not obliged to declare that fact. If you buy something from such an auctioneer, the amount you pay will be when your bid reaches the level where he is content to take that margin of profit. He might have bought that item from a dealer the week before and 'auction' it at two or even ten times the cost price, and there's nothing illegal in that. It's just that he didn't happen to mention that to you in the front of the catalogue, or you might have been less keen to bid.

What is written in great detail in the small print of most auction catalogues is a disclaimer of responsibility for the accuracy of items catalogued. It would be unfair of me to single out an actual example of such wording, which might be recognizable, as each auction house tries to wrap up the phraseology in such a legally tight manner as to be action-proof. What they say in effect is that their description of an item represents merely their opinion as to age, genuineness or attribution, and that they cannot be held responsible if such description proves inaccurate. In other words: this is what we think such and such a lot is, but we may be wrong, so don't take it as fact as we are not 'responsible' for our opinion. It has never ceased to amaze me that they can get away with this, the more so since very often in the small print is a section advising potential clients on how to get in touch with their 'experts' for 'expert' advice!

If you should find yourself in the unfortunate position of having bought something at auction which proves not to be what you understood by the catalogue description, in other words, if you feel you have been deceived, your best step is to first take it up with the auctioneer, who might see fit to refund your money.

If he proves difficult, get in touch straight away with the Trading Standards Office at your local council offices, where you need to speak to one of their 'enforcers'. If they are in any doubt about their powers in making auctioneers abide by the same law that applies to all other traders, then you might point out to them the result of a recent High Court case (Queen's Bench Division, 11th June 1990, Derbyshire County Council v Vincent). Here the High Court ruled that salerooms were not exempt from Section 1(1)(a) of the Trade Descriptions Act, whereby any person, who, in the course of a trade or business, applies a false trade description to any goods, shall ... be guilty of an offence. An auctioneer cannot 'contract out' of his obligations by any disclaimer in his conditions of sale. Furthermore it is no defence to claim that it was not known that the description was false.

Before you get into such complications, however, you must first learn how to understand auction catalogue descriptions. We will see later how you can read between the lines in an auction catalogue, but in the meantime let us look at another source of goods for sale in auction rooms.

If you are bidding at auction on items that are not owned by the auctioneer himself, where do the goods come from that are on offer? You might imagine, indeed you are often led to imagine, that the items are the property of private individuals who for whatever reason are having a clear out. This is often the case, but in almost any auction a good proportion of the items on offer may be trade items, that is goods that have been put in the auction by a dealer in those goods. Some dealers may even conduct the majority of their selling via auction houses rather than an antique shop. There is nothing wrong with doing this, but it might be more honourable for an auctioneer to indicate which items in his sale are trade entries – though I don't know any that do.

Some catalogues mark with an asterisk any items subject to VAT, and one would deduce that those were items put in by a dealer. Such a deduction would probably be correct, but most dealers do not pay VAT as a separate item. The majority of them pay under the Special Scheme, and therefore do not show VAT separately. Therefore items from nearly all dealers selling through an auction would not carry an asterisk and cannot be identified in any way.

Of course, if the public at large knew that some items in an auction were trade goods put there by dealers to sell at a profit, they might well be reluctant to bid, or bid as highly, on those goods. This applies particularly to those innocent members of the public whose very purpose in attending an auction sale may have arisen through the mistaken impression that they were bidding for private goods.

But what about a 'country house' sale, you may ask. Surely in those instances the contents on offer *are* the contents of the house. Well, they may be, but perhaps not items *exclusively* from that house because for the most part even country house sales are 'salted' with trade goods if for no other reason than to make up any deficiency of the variety of goods originating from the house. Of course, every auctioneer knows that the public are more likely to believe they are bidding for private goods in a country house sale than in the regular auction room. Some auctioneers may designate in their catalogue those items that are in the house sale and did not originate from there, but most don't. They simply leave you to assume that all the contents are purely original to the house's last owner.

So if your thinking runs along the lines that an auction sale is somehow likely to be the source of untouched items that have not seen the light of day for years, think again. Such an item, which may not have been on the market for many years (fifty to a hundred or more) is known in the trade as a 'sleeper' or a 'sleepy' item. These are usually well thought of by the trade because they are items which have not been 'got at'. A sleeper is sometimes identified by the layer of dust on it, particularly on the clock movement. Bear in mind, however, that dealers may well dust up a clock before putting it into a sale in order to give it the look of a sleeper.

A recently cleaned clock appearing in a sale tends to be off-putting to the trade as it may have been done up to sell, or have serious mechanical problems not immediately obvious. If you're thinking of selling one yourself by auction, don't restore it first. The fact that it may not be in working order will not usually put off a serious buyer, but cleaning it might.

If buying a clock at auction bear in mind that you have no guarantee of any kind that the clock is genuine or in working order. Even if, as sometimes happens, an auctioneer introducing the lot might comment that this clock seems to be in working order and it nevertheless proves not to be, you have no redress. He will not stand by such a statement unless he stipulates this in the catalogue, and I don't recall ever seeing a catalogue description specify that one was in working order.

So if Mr Auctioneer specifies in his preamble to a particular lot that the clock is in full working order, why not call out and ask him if he guarantees that. Auctioneers are people and you are allowed to speak to them or ask them a question if you wish, though few people do out of embarrassment at speaking out in front of a large audience. By and large, however, auctioneers are not people to give guarantees, and my bet is that he will either withdraw his statement at once or pretend he has not heard you. You can draw your own conclusion from this. More often he will make some guarded remark such as that it appears to be working now, was working in the house when they collected it, or that it seems all right to him, none of which statements constitute any guarantee. If he thinks he has been caught out, he will quite likely make some jocular quip to get the audience on his side and to shut you up. Remember auctioneers spend half their lives on stage and they are often masters at entertaining an audience and at disciplining an unruly bidder. So if he tries to put you down, you will know why and be able to judge for yourself his degree of confidence in the clock.

Another point to remember is that auctioneers sell everything. His last item may have been a Tibetan umbrella stand and his next one a stuffed Galapagos penguin, and he probably knows no more about clocks than he does about either of those. On the other hand, he will often introduce a clock as being one that he knows to be 'a good clock', when he would not know what constituted a good clock if it fell on him. He knows that and you know it too in the cold light of day, but in the heat of the auction even the most pathetically transparent statement hovers in your ear and may well influence you. Think about it – did you ever see an auctioneer introduce a clock as being one he knew to be a bad one? So if intending to buy a clock at auction, forget about guarantees of any kind because there are none, as auctioneers take pains to tell you in expensively purchased legal terminology in the catalogue small print.

There are other factors to take into consideration as well. Even the most honourable auctioneer has a problem with a clock, in that most clocks are the product of more than one individual workman. The most obvious example perhaps is with a longcase clock where the case, even if original to the clock, was made by a different craftsman anyway, and very often the dial was also. So such a clock is a combined product of three separate craftsmen. It is usually possible for an expert to be able to recognize whether these three original parts began life together and have remained together ever since. It is very important to the true value of the clock that all three should belong together. Auctioneers cannot be expected to be experts at everything, however, and most have only the most basic knowledge of clocks. This means they have no idea whether the clock is genuine or married up and therefore they cannot specify this in their catalogues. Some auctioneers do have some degree of knowledge of this subject, but find it convenient to pretend not to, so that they can vaguely let any clock pass as all-original without actually saying so. They could in any case deny responsibility for this 'opinion', as we have already seen.

On the other hand, there are auctioneers who do know about

Detail of a very fine mahogany clock of about 1790 by Thomas Scott of Gainsborough. Plus points: handsomely proportioned pagoda top style, beautiful inlay work and stringing, original spire finials, Corinthian brass capitals to hood pillars and trunk quarter-pillars, original hands, centre calendar.

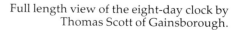

Full length view of the eight-day clock by Thomas Scott of Gainsborough.

clocks and who make efforts in their cataloguing to specify when they think one is of doubtful originality. They use such terms as 'made-up' or 'married' to indicate this. Another way of saying this is to record it as 'part seventeenth century', or 'partly nineteenth century', etc., which is their way of saying a considerable part of it is not as old as that. At least these auctioneers are trying to be fair with the buyer in pointing out instances where originality is in doubt.

Other terms used by some are expressions such as 'the associated case', or 'the associated movement'. This expression does not mean what you might innocently take it to mean, namely 'the case with it'. Quite the opposite, this term means that the auctioneer is pointing out to you that, in his opinion, the case does *not* belong, but has been 'associated' (in the sense of being put together with it) at a later time, maybe even last week! So auctioneers who do this are quietly tipping you off without making some condemnatory remark which would put off everyone. Anything in auctioneering terms which is described as 'associated' means non-original.

With auctioneers who do understand clocks the position can often be even more complicated. This is because we soon get into the realms of not only clocks which might be made up from parts of others (i.e. associated) but of names. Names might be genuine signatures or fakes, clocks might be genuine but with faked signatures, clocks might be fakes with faked signatures, clocks might be made as copies in the style of older ones they imitate, and so on. Here some auctioneers may also try to tip you off in various ways, but you need to understand the terminology.

A reproduction clock is often visibly just that, and many auctioneers will stipulate this fact. Grandmother and grand-daughter clocks are mostly modern anyway (say within the last 100 years), so an auctioneer might well call them by these names rather than mention any period. No mention of age, usually means the item has no great age. If you happen to believe that grandmother and granddaughter clocks are antique, the auctioneer will probably leave you undisturbed in your belief. (For further discussion of these types see Chapter 8). An auctioneer will not fail to mention the age of an antique clock through oversight. Use of such a word as 'old' indicates deliberate vagueness on his part and means no more than 'not new'.

Sometimes a clock will be described using the word 'style', and this word means different things in different circumstances. A quite valid use may be in describing a clockcase as being, for instance, one of 'Chippendale style', which means just what it says without imparting any suggestion of Chippendale quality or age. Though a novice may in innocence wrongly believe that it is of that quality or age. It is quite possible for a 1920s clock to be described as being in 'Chippendale style' whilst being made in plywood! So read a catalogue description with caution because the auctioneer has carefully chosen his words from all those available to him.

The other and more slippery use of the word 'style' is when an item is described as being in 'eighteenth-century style', which does not mean it is an eighteenth-century clock, quite the contrary. If it was an eighteenth-century one, or he thought it was, he would say just that, even though his small print warned you not to rely on his beliefs. By inserting the word 'style' the auctioneer is telling you discreetly that it is not eighteenth century in anything but 'style'. In all probability it is modern, though he usually does not bother to add that word.

Let's invent an example. 'An Edwardian Chippendale style longcase clock' means a 1910 clock with Chippendale 'influence'. 'A mahogany longcase clock in eighteenth-century style with Chippendale features' means the same thing. You must not interpret this as an eighteenth-century mahogany longcase clock with Chippendale features.

Names are even more confusing. 'An eighteenth-century oak longcase clock by Thomas Lister of Halifax' tells you that in the auctioneer's opinion the clock is by that maker. 'An eighteenth-century oak longcase clock, the dial signed "Thomas Lister, Halifax" may tell you that he is uncertain as to the genuineness of the signature or clock. 'An eighteenth-century oak longcase clock, the name on the dial "Thomas Lister, Halifax" may tell you the same thing. Some auctioneers may use the term 'the name engraved on the dial' or 'the name inscribed on the dial' as alternatives to 'signed'. Whilst others may mean quite different things by these different wordings. Each auctioneer (or cataloguer) has his own 'style' of wording and whilst he no doubt knows what he means by it, you probably don't unless you are a regular at his auctions.

In any event it's not worth too much head scratching, because the auctioneer has already told you that whatever his catalogue description may say is only his opinion and is not to be confused with or taken for fact.

Another word to watch out for is 'attributed'. For example: 'A mahogany longcase clock of the mid eighteenth century by Robert Parkinson of Lancaster, the case attributed to Gillow of Lancaster.' In case you don't know the name, Gillows were a famous cabinetmaking firm in Lancaster and their work was of high quality. The clock world is suffering from a recent outbreak of Gillowitis, whereby everyone tries to get in on the Gillow act and squeeze extra financial mileage out of the name. It is amazing the variety of clockcases which are 'attributed' to Gillows when there is not the faintest shadow of a Gillow hand in the making of them. The important factor in an item 'attributed' to let us say Gillows, is the person who 'attributes' it, and, as we know, an auctioneer denies responsibility for any attribution he makes. So an 'attribution' such as that in the above catalogue entry is worthless and no more than padding intended to 'attribute' more value to the clock.

As it happens Gillows did not mark their clockcases in any way, so nobody can prove or disprove whether it is by them, and anyone can make such an 'attribution' to any case at all without fear of being proved wrong. If you come across a case attributed to Gillows, or any other cabinetmaker for that matter, you have only to ask what evidence exists for that attribution and you will probably find that the answer is none.

In summarizing one can say no more than that a catalogue description usually means less than it says, never more. Cataloguers have developed that refined political and literary talent of being 'sparing with the truth'.

Many auction catalogues will give an estimate of the expected price, usually a very vague estimate. Such an estimate might show a range such as £400 to £600, £2,000 to £3,000, or even £2,000 to £4,000. Obviously auctioneers cannot predict the heights of folly to which two competing bidders might go in the heat of an auction battle, so one cannot entirely blame the auctioneer of a small auction house or the 'expert' of a larger one if on the day the auction price reaches ten times the expert estimate. There is more to it than that, however, and those who set the estimates are not as inept as they might sometimes make themselves out to be. Auction estimates are almost always set low, deliberately low, and there is a very definite reason for it.

Most people reading an auction catalogue also read the estimate, especially if it is a clock which might interest them. Even the experienced cannot help failing to notice a tempting low estimate. The inexperienced reads the catalogue, for which he may have paid the price of a hardback book, as if it were a mail order catalogue, and is struck by the number of bargains on offer. The low estimate has a bearing on whether the experienced and the novice will be drawn to attend the sale. Too high an estimate will result in bidders being put off and not attending. Once the sale begins, the punters who were drawn in by the low estimates may well keep bidding to the point where the original estimate is only a distant memory.

Let me illustrate an example. An auctioneer some 150 miles away telephoned me one time to tip me off about a nice clock coming up shortly, which he thought might be in my line. If I had been naïve I might have wondered why he had rung *me*, as someone who had never attended his auctions and never met him. Why had he singled me out of all the dealers in the yearbooks with this red hot tip? The clock he described would certainly have been of interest to me at the figure he 'thought' it would bring, which was £4,000 to £6,000, since I could tell from his description that it was at least a £10,000 clock. A day or two later I was chatting to a friend who deals in furniture and the occasional clock, and sure enough this enterprising auctioneer had phoned him up too about this same clock, but had told him it might bring £2,000 to £4,000 – and that was *after* he had told me £4,000 to £6,000. We both smiled about this, as we understood that the reason for the lower estimate to him, was that, as he was a dealer less likely to buy a clock, he had to make it sound a more obvious bargain to draw him there. We guessed that the auctioneer had probably spent the whole day telephoning every dealer who might be remotely interested in buying that clock. Neither of us went to the sale, but the clock sold for £16,000 as two dealers from the other end of the country battled it out, having travelled 400 miles to do so.

It is sometimes thought that the estimates in a catalogue give an indication of the clock's reserve price, that is the price below which the auctioneer has been instructed not to sell. This may be true some of the time, but some auctioneers rely on the buyer's assumption that a lower estimate is a reserve figure. Therefore an estimate of let's say £2,000 to £3,000 suggests that the reserve is £2,000. That's what you might think, and that's what they know you might think.

An example of how this may not be the case occurred recently. It happened that a clock I had sold some years previously to a collector come up for auction and it was estimated in the catalogue at £4,000 to £6,000. The implication being that once £4,000 was passed, it was for sale. I was puzzled that the owner had not offered the clock back to me, as I would have bought it happily within those price levels, and perhaps grudgingly at £7,000. I was even more puzzled as I knew the owner reasonably well and had been chatting to him only a week or two earlier. He could have had my offer on his clock for the asking, could perhaps have sold it sooner with no commission to pay and for a higher price than he might get at auction. I didn't go to the auction as I felt suspicious. In the event the clock didn't sell and was bought in in excess of £8,000. I later found out that the reserve was £9,000. So again the same old principle in catalogue estimates can be seen to be to 'price low'.

Strangely enough only a matter of days after I had written the above, there appeared a report in the press which stated that to give an estimate which is below the reserve figure may in fact be illegal. Under Section 20 of the Consumer Protection Act it is an offence to give 'any consumer an indication which is misleading as to the price at which any goods are available'. Trading standards officers are pondering the matter at present, but current thinking seems to run along the lines that it might well be an offence against a private buyer but not against a dealer, since the Act refers to a person buying for private use. It seems a very strange state of affairs to me if the laws of the land appear to apply to some vendors and not others and to some buyers and not others. What if I as a dealer want to buy an item for my own 'private use'?

A *very* low auctioneer's estimate may be a clue that the auctioneer thinks the clock is wrong. If we imagine a clock which common sense would price at say £1,000, a normal low estimate might be £600 to £700 which is low enough to be tempting. Such a clock estimated at £300 to £400 is probably an indication that it is a dud and the auctioneers are tipping you off.

Let us suppose you plan to bid on a clock you have examined at the auction preview, which normally takes place on the day (or two days) before the sale proper. You have a choice of several ways of going about this, and the distance involved in travelling to the auction may well influence the manner you chose to adopt. You can go to the sale yourself and stand there till your appropriate lot appears and bid by raising your hand, scratching your nose, or by raising the 'paddle', which is a new system some of the larger auction rooms have recently introduced. Alternatively you can arrange to bid by telephone, provided you book in advance with the auctioneer, so that they can call you when they get within a few lots of yours. It may be a village hall with no phone facilities, of course. Most provincial auctions will have a limited number of phone lines available, however. Phone bidding is more convenient but no less nerve-racking than bidding in the room. You will have to try and make sure your own line is free for about an hour either side of the estimated time your lot will come up. The bidding rate can vary as an auctioneer might get through anywhere between 60 and 100 lots in an hour, or more, so guessing the time of your awaited call is tricky.

Another method is to leave your bid with the auctioneer, and this is known as bidding 'on the book' or leaving a bid 'on the book'. What this means, in effect, is that you decide what your top bid is to be and leave that figure with the auctioneer. Let us suppose the estimate is £700 to £1,000 and you decide your top bid is to be £900. Most auctions also charge a buyer's 'premium' which is an additional percentage on top of the bid, often 10%. Additionally they have to charge you VAT on the premium. So if you buy the clock at £900 you will actually pay £900 plus £90 premium plus £15.75 VAT (currently 17½%) and your clock will cost you £1,005.75. It is very easy to forget to include the premium as an additional cost when mentally calculating how much you want to pay as a top bid, and of course the premium and VAT apply regardless of what method of bidding you use.

But bidding 'on the book' is more complicated than that, and it brings in the whole question of who you are bidding against. In all auctions you are bidding against the auctioneer in the first place and any other bidders in the second. An auctioneer will 'pick bids off the wall' until he gets enough response. If he gets no bids, or none high enough, he will usually still appear to 'sell' the clock to a buyer no one but he could see (since he does not exist). He will call out some name or other and the clerk will write that item down to the invisible, non-existent bidder. In other words, the clock has failed to sell and has been bought in. To save face, however, the auctioneer has gone through the pretence of selling it.

If the auctioneer has your book bid, he will run the price to the point where he passes the reserve, bidding off the wall if he needs to, and the real bidding starts when your money comes into play. If he was honourable and if the reserve was £500, then with nobody else bidding you should in theory buy the clock at your next bid, say £550. A few auctioneers do this, but not many.

More often the auctioneer takes the view that you have left him a firm bid of £900 and he is justified to run the price up to that figure. So with a book bid you might find you have bought a clock at £900 plus premium plus VAT, when if you had been in the room yourself you might have bought it for £550, because you may have been the only bidder. That's the big chance you take in leaving a bid on the book. Dealers do this regularly because they take the view that they are happy with the clock at the bid level they have left. I don't often leave book bids but when I do, if I get the clock at all, it is almost always on my top bid. You soon learn to judge which system an auctioneer works on.

If you leave a book bid, the auctioneer must stop bidding (for you) on your bid figure. If he gets off on the wrong foot, as they describe it, it might be that some other bidder calls out your figure of £900. Later you will find the clock sold at your bid price, but you didn't get it. The way to avoid that happening is to leave your bid as £900 'plus one', which means plus one extra bid if yours should fall wrong-footed. Some people like to leave a bid 'plus two'.

A better idea, if you can arrange it, is to get a friend to bid for you if you have one who lives closer to the auction than you.

Many items in an auction may be stock put in from dealers. Sometimes at an auction I can recognize some of the clocks there because I've seen them for sale in antique shops. Some dealers who find an item sticking will try it in an auction, where the public may get carried away and may often pay more than they would for similar items in an antique shop. A dealer I know had a pair of vases in his shop window for a year priced at £1,800 without selling them. He then tried them in an auction and they sold for just under £3,000 only a few miles from where he had displayed them unsuccessfully for a year at almost half that price.

A dealer who has put items into an auction will himself often attend that auction to try and force up the bids on his piece. It can be a risky move, but many do it successfully. This is because a private buyer may often recognize a dealer and think to himself that if the dealer is still bidding, then the price must still be all right, so he too can keep bidding.

Where an auctioneer fails to get a high enough bid (or even any bid at all), he will usually pick imaginary bids off the wall in an attempt to arouse some interest. This is dangerous practice for him as he may well be left bidding alone at an ever-escalating level. When this happens he has two choices. He can pretend to sell the clock and knock it down to a fictitious name, or he can admit defeat and knock it down as withdrawn. An auctioneer may adopt either of these practices according to the situation.

The naïve onlooker may mistakenly believe the clock has sold at what may appear to be a very low price, a bargain in fact. Anyone inexperienced in auction ways may read a newspaper report of some of the prices realized and get a completely false impression of bargains galore, when in fact as many as 25% of the lots in the sale may have failed to sell.

I saw a particularly distinctive longcase in an auction, not long ago, which had previously been offered around the trade without success by the owner, who was a dealer. The price asked had been around £1,400, but was negotiable as he wanted rid of it. The auctioneer was bidding away to around the thousand level, when bidding slowed to a standstill. The owner was in the room to observe the outcome, and hopefully to go home wealthier. The auctioneer pleaded for any further bids or he would withdraw the lot, but no further bids came. He began to repeat his withdrawal threat when the owner could stand the tension no longer and called from the audience: 'Sell it, sell it!' The auctioneer promptly knocked down his hammer and pronounced the lot as withdrawn. The old hands in the room burst into laughter, because what was obvious to them, if not to the owner, was that the auctioneer hadn't yet raised a single bid.

Bidding 'rings' operate at many auction rooms. A ring is the term used where several dealers (it could be two or twenty) agree jointly not to bid against each other so that an item may sell to one of their ring at a low price. They will then auction the lot between themselves after the sale, and that way everyone in the ring gets a payout according to his bid strength, and the one who finally buys the item saves to some degree over what he would have had to pay out if he had bought it against the competition. Rings are against the law, but difficult to prove. Those in the ring all gain. The vendor loses and the auctioneer loses as he gets his commission on a lower sale price than he might have achieved without the ring operating.

If you and a friend agree together not to bid against each other at an auction, nobody could claim that constituted a ring. If two dealers who are friends do the same, is that a ring or not, and can it be proved in court?

One strong bidder outside the ring may well cause the price to reach its normal level anyway, and this often happens. But as a naïve bystander you do not know whether a price realized at an auction is a ring price or a real price. You might see or hear about a clock apparently sold for £500 which unknown to you was ringed and later sold in the ring for £5,000. This could be sold to a different dealer a day or two later and perhaps be seen on sale in his showroom soon after at £6,000. That may appear to you to be an outrageous profit margin because you don't know the story behind the price, and you could have been at that auction yourself with £5,000 in your hand and failed to buy the clock. So you will begin to see the point I made earlier that auctions are as much illusion as reality.

If you decide to bid on a clock to a level high enough to buy it, the presence of a ring in the room would make no difference, and you would be unaware of the ring presence anyway. I've seen determined and wealthy private bidders who are intent on buying a particular clock regardless of the price. Such a bidder might think that if the trade are bidding against him, as they almost always are whether he knows it or not, he has bought the clock at an acceptable price (a price 'the trade' was willing to run to anyway). He could, however, be quite wrong in thinking so, as he may have been bidding against the owner of the clock who was chancing his luck, or against a dealer who had a very special reason to bid strongly on that one (perhaps for a particularly wealthy client). So by following a dealer's lead (false or otherwise) the buyer may have paid several times the real value of the clock.

It happened to me once that I had a commission to buy a particular clock for a client, which should have fallen for about £2,000 or a little over, but my instructions were to buy it regardless of price with an insanity limit of £5,000 total cost to the client including my fee. I dropped out at £4,800 when the balance left for me would not have covered my petrol money, and it turned out the buyer was a local millionaire who fancied that clock regardless of cost, and who would, if need be, have paid twice that price. The clock, of course, was not worth the price it sold for, but any spectator who was a novice would simply assume that was the price level such a clock would normally bring.

To be able to see inside a longcase movement you need good lighting, or ideally a small pocket torch. A torch should in any case be carried at all times by a potential clock buyer, as you are going to want to look in dark places such as inside the case of a longcase, where normal lighting is inadequate. Some dealers may have the clock standing in a dark corner so that your view is deliberately hampered. 'Private' sellers are notorious for this, sometimes going as far as taking the bulb out of the hall lamp and pretending it is not working. If you carry a torch you not only overcome this problem, but you get the additional pleasure of seeing the vendor's face drop when you produce it. Auctioneers can be amongst the worst offenders of all as they will often wedge a clock tight between a chest of drawers on one side and a wardrobe at the other with maybe a settee across the front. In such a situation you cannot even see the clock at all from midway down and this is done deliberately so that you cannot see damage, woodworm, rot, splitting, miscolouring or even missing panels on the clock base. The solution is to ask to move, or have moved, the furniture obscuring your view, and if they refuse, you know perfectly well why.

If you have difficulty viewing the case of a longcase, then getting a good view of the movement may be almost impossible, especially if the seatboard height is above eye level. In those cases ask to see the movement out of the case or ask for a buffet to stand on so that you can see it. If you ask a porter you may get nothing but grumbles or excuses, so ask the auctioneer or the person in charge of the viewing.

When you view a longcase at an auction preview, you need to know beforehand just what you are going to look at and why. First of all, you will judge the overall clock in its case, whether you like the look of the wood, the colour and the style. You will also want to know the height relative to your own headroom at home, and it is quite possible that the height may not be indicated in the catalogue (if there is one). In a village hall the ceilings could be 30 feet high and even a tall clock can look deceptively small. I've learned from experience that when I stretch my hand fully upwards, I can just touch 7 ft. 6 in. Measure your own reach-height, then you can always guess how much above or below your reach the clock is and therefore work out the approximate height quite closely.

You will want to look inside the case by removing the hood so that you can judge whether the clock belongs to that case by the state of the seatboard housing (see Chapter 8) and other things. If you are anxious about breaking something, or if you, can't reach, ask the auctioneer to do it for you. Some auctioneers tie the hoods on to the clocks with string, or tie the whole thing to the post of a marquee, and you will need to ask them to untie it so that you can examine it. They know perfectly well that you want to, but may feign ignorance of the fact thereby hoping to induce the foolish to bid without looking inside. I've seen people, dealers even, suddenly come to life during a sale and bid on a clock they had not intended to bid on perhaps because the price seems to be temptingly low. When the lot is being auctioned you have of course missed your chance to inspect it, and I've seen dealers buy a 'bargain' clock only to find later the clock dial had an electric movement behind it, or even no movement at all.

You should also want to look inside the body of the case with your torch, because the inside may reveal old apple boxes and other amazing truths usually hidden in gloom. Sometimes at auction you will find the case door locked and the key missing, so ask someone to unlock it for you as you do need to see inside. Door keys and winding keys are often removed by the auctioneers and kept in a safe place, since people often steal such things from auction rooms, if left on view.

If you are viewing a bracket clock at auction, it is often quite impossible to see anything of the movement unless the case has glass side panels, which some have. The auctioneer is normally willing to allow someone he feels is competent (which may not be you) to remove the movement from its case in order to examine it. If you are capable of doing this, then you'll need to take a small screwdriver with you to remove the bracket screws holding it in.

Longcase clocks are the easiest of any to examine before buying. Bracket clocks are more tricky and require more experience. Lantern clocks are very difficult and really outside the scope of a novice. For a beginner to buy a lantern clock at auction is a risky business. They have been subject to faking and alteration for many years. Half the experienced dealers in the land are wary of buying lantern clocks at auction, and for a beginner to do so, he must be either very brave or very foolish. English dial clocks (fusee wall clocks, that is) are not hard to examine, provided that you know how to remove the wooden restraining pegs which hold on the front of the case. Doing this with a clock eight feet high on an auction room wall while balanced on one toe on a shaky chair jostled by passing viewers is an acquired skill, but if you don't look inside, you don't know what you are buying, and there may be nothing at all inside the case!

In a shop the dealer can quite easily show you the movements of any type of clock. With trickier items such as lantern clocks he can probably explain to you any modifications it has undergone during its long and perhaps complicated life. At an auction you are on your own.

If you buy a longcase clock at auction check whether it has a weight or weights, a pendulum, a winding key and a door key, because quite often these things are missing.

10   Values and Prices

Prices are a very difficult aspect to discuss in any book, which is why so few try. There are several reasons for this, not least being that prices are out of date by the time the book is printed and can look ludicrous two or three years on. Another is that in the end each clock is a unique item, which may resemble others in greater or lesser degree, but is not the same as any other clock in the world. The danger in giving guides towards prices or values is that the beginner sees clock A priced at £5,000, then sees clock B, which may be completely different, but which to him in his inexperience looks exactly the same, and concludes that clock B is also worth £5,000. The experienced enthusiast does not need the price guide anyway and can recognize for himself the difference between A and B.

When the beginner asks a question such as 'How much are longcases bringing these days?' he is asking a question that cannot be answered. It is the same as asking: how much are houses bringing these days, or what does a car cost these days? Even if the question was confined to detached houses, detached houses with a garden or detached houses with a garden and two bathrooms, the problem remains.

The answer cannot even be that this kind of oak longcase or this kind of longcase with a brass dial in mahogany brings £x, because none of these definitions pins down the details adequately to price anything but a particular clock in question. So before I attempt the impossible task of discussing prices, let's look at it from the other end for a moment and think about what price you *can't* buy a clock for.

Quite often these days I find myself in the position where the phone rings with a general enquiry from a potential customer looking at clocks for the first time. He has put together a sum of money with which to buy himself a longcase clock. What can I offer him for £500? The answer is nothing! That is perhaps a blow to him, since £500 is a tidy sum. It is also a blow to me, as I'm turning away £500 worth of business. So what about £1,000? The answer is the same. What about £1,500 or £2,000? Well, within this price range I can show him just a few items, but his choice will be very limited. What is more, by the time this book is printed the answer will probably be that I can't offer anything under £2,000.

Before this price is arrived at I have probably already spent in excess of £300 on restoration of clock and case and sometimes much more. Restoration, together with subsequent testing, can mean a time lapse between my buying a clock and offering it for sale of two to three months. A buyer looking at a clock in unrestored state needs to bear this in mind and also the fact that it can cost just as much to restore a cheap clock as a costly one.

On the other hand, there *are* longcase clocks to be bought for under £1,500, £1,000 and quite possibly under £500. We've all seen such clocks for sale and someone does eventually buy them. They are not, however, the kind of clock I want to put my money into because they fall into my reject slot of being married, altered, ugly, poor quality or just plain poor sellers for any of a hundred different reasons. Those who buy clocks in this price range will think I am being snobbish in my attitude. Those whose sights are set higher will think I'm an idiot even to consider buying at this lower price level. Each collector, and more so each dealer, today has his own particular slot in the market which forces him into a particular price range.

There are dealers who stock nothing at less than £10,000. Some, not many, sell clocks in the £30,000 plus range and higher. Some start at £5,000 and others at £500. These people are not simply selling the same level of goods with different price tickets on them. They are selling at quite different rungs of quality in the price ladder. Of course, we would all like to buy at £500 and sell at £5,000, but it just does not happen that way, or at least I'm looking forward to the first time it happens to me.

Less than a year ago I was offered a big thirty-hour 'Yorkshire' longcase made in my own village in the 1840s for £175. It was a perfectly genuine clock though in miserable condition and I turned it down. Yet I could have bought it, restored it and offered it for sale to a customer who wanted a lower-priced clock, even though restoration would have worked out at more than the clock's cost. I didn't because past experience has taught me that whilst most customers very much like the idea of buying something at a low price level, when they see what a low price ticket offers, it's a very different reaction. The last thing I want is a clock, however cheaply priced, that is TUS – totally unsaleable!

On the other hand, a customer appeared one day, who stands out very clearly in my mind. He wanted a longcase, but would consider nothing over £2,000 – not an unreasonable attitude. I showed him what I had. He then asked the price of a much better example, which was £4,500. 'Right,' he said, 'I'll have that one!'

I pointed out that he had just told me to exclude everything over £2,000, but his answer was that having seen that one had completely changed his way of thinking. Quality speaks for itself, even to a novice, who, one might think, would be blind to quality by virtue of being unaccustomed to studying it. In the end the quality is more important than the price.

Any illustration of a clock, such as those in this book, will show its shape, style, proportion, age, woods, type of dial, length of duration and height. All these are very important factors and from them we can assess the kind of price range such a clock would fall into. These factors alone are not enough, however. The all important aspects, which make or break it in terms of price (once the foregoing points are established) are condition, colour and finish (patina, if you like). These cannot be seen in any picture.

In a certain sense one can judge the beginnings of 'condition' from a photograph, because case damage, splitting, shrinking, shaken joints and scratching can all to some limited extent be made out from a photograph, but only in a negative sense. What the picture would show is essentially only damage, and perhaps even then only to a trained eye. Repairs and replacements are seldom easy to spot in a picture unless they are in an obviously incorrect style.

For any given clock the condition can vary from poor and average to magnificent. Most will fall roughly in the middle. It is quite possible, however, to take an example that might commonly sell at around £3,000, and find that an exceptional example of this item will bring £4,000 and a mediocre one £2,000. This is common sense to everyone, though beginners do not always realize this and the gap between poor and superb can be even wider. Nor do beginners always realize that a mediocre clock may be so mediocre that it may not sell at all! Most people, dealers included, would rather pay a little more for a good example than save money and buy a poor one, which they might, ever after, regret having bought. So the bottom end of the market (in terms of condition) may not be simply a bit cheaper than the next level up the condition scale, but could be such as to put off any buyer totally, or at least any experienced buyer or dealer.

The novice may feel that it is of no importance that a dealer would not buy such a clock, because he is not concerned with what a dealer will buy or will not buy. In fact dealers are desperately keen to buy anything within their affordable price range, and if a dealer will not buy a clock at any price, that is quite simply because that clock is no good – in commercial terms, of course. A dealer's very livelihood depends on his ability to sift the wheat from the chaff and a dealer's opinion is usually a highly accurate reflection of the commercial market. So the novice who buys an item that no dealer wants may be content with the wisdom of his decision until such time comes that he tries to sell it again, or part-exchange it for a better one.

An example of this very situation happened to me the day after I wrote the above paragraph. A couple arrived hoping to see a clock they might buy with a view to trading in their present one as a part-exchange. Was I willing to do that? Well, yes, in principle, but what I would not do was to take in something I did not want and could not sell in exchange for something I thought I could. That sounded fair enough to them and they were viewing a handsome clock in the £3,500 region, in which they were quite interested. They admitted at once that the clocks they were looking at were in a class beyond their own, but after all that was why they wanted to trade up.

I had a fair suspicion what was coming next as soon as they began to describe their clock and its maker. It was a monstrous Victorian thirty-hour clock, and I knew immediately that it was something I did not want at any price even if it had been in mint condition, which of course they never are anyway. If I wanted to I could buy clocks such as theirs every day of the week at £300 to £400. The difficulty was in telling them that, in letting them down as lightly as possible.

I suggested that their clock was not the type I bought and that whilst I would be delighted to sell them a clock, I did not want theirs in part-exchange at any price. I intimated that perhaps the best thing was for them to put their clock in auction somewhere near to its town of making, where maybe they would have competition from people who valued the fact that the clock was local more than its individual merits. I indicated that their clock might bring between £400 and £600. They left totally unable to comprehend why their clock was worth so little and mine so much. They could see the difference, but could not begin to comprehend the price difference. Yet they drove away in their £30,000 car, and could well have seen why that was worth £30,000 alongside one worth £3,000.

I doubt if I shall ever see them again because I happened to be the unfortunate one to disillusion them about the value of their own clock. If they had been to see an auctioneer first and had received the bad news from him, then I might have had a chance. I don't know how much they had paid for their clock, but the

Thirteen-inch dial of the clock by Pim of Bideford clearly showing the rocking ship. Plus features: restrained dial style, rocking ship, original hands.

Eight-day longcase dating from about 1840 by J.R. Pim of Bideford in Devon in pine case. Plus points: small height (about 7 ft. 3 in.), very clean condition, rocking ship.

moral of the story is that if you buy cheap you may find you've bought something that nobody else wanted it. As my abbreviating friend would say: TUS, totally unsaleable!

I shall never forget a classic conversation which took place one day in my showroom and which neatly summarizes the attitude of many an inexperienced paddler in the shallow end of the clock pool. A couple were drawn immediately to one particular clock because, they said, it was 'exactly' like their own. The only difference according to the wife was that theirs was in mahogany. The husband insisted it was oak. It was, according to the wife, seven feet tall. The husband disagreed and said it was eight before it had been sawn off halfway across the base. The wife disagreed because, she pointed out, it was only the feet that had been sawn off. She added that, on the other hand, the horns had been broken off, but the husband again stepped in to say that, if she remembered, he had made some new horns and had glued them on, so that didn't count.

By this time my patience was waning and in any case it was of no interest to me how much they had sawn off or nailed on, because it was very obvious that the clock they were describing was what we call in the trade an absolute dog! I ventured to say that judging by what they were saying, their clock was nothing like mine at all. 'Oh, yes it is,' they both agreed. 'It's exactly like that!' I knew what was coming next. They asked how much mine was. When I told them they were both amazed and, as they left, they remarked that they had no idea their clock was so valuable and they would have to increase the insurance cover!

Where the problem arises is that every seller tends to mentally place his example in the highest grade and every buyer places it in the lowest. People believe in the end what they want to believe and beginners, in particular, have difficulty coming to terms with the fact that they have just seen one clock at £2,000 and another, which to them seems almost identical, at £4,000. This is another reason why any discussion of prices is fraught with difficulties.

There are two books which are 'price guides', Miller's and Lyle's (Miller's *Antiques Price Guide* and *The Lyle Official Antiques Review*). As well as other antiques, they show illustrations of clocks, state the origin, dealer, auction, etc. and give a guide to its price. The novice may find these books helpful, and they are published annually with new examples each year. The reader must carefully read the introductory text to distinguish what the prices mean. In other words, are they auction estimates, realized auction prices, a dealer's retail price, a dealer's estimated retail price range or an estimated retail price based on the auction price plus an allowance for restoration and profit margin? Bear in mind too that most books take months to prepare and more months before they are published, so prices might already be a year in arrears by the time the book is released.

Many people unfamiliar with longcase clocks are afraid of the size, especially the height. They are concerned the clock may be too tall for their particular house or may be overpowering and dominating. When you think about it, the dial of a clock is unlikely to stand higher on your wall than a picture would hang, so for most people this fear of height is unwarranted. Nevertheless it is there, and often they insist on a height lower than they need and will have to pay a premium for doing so. Because, if other things were equal (which we know with most clocks they hardly ever are) then a smaller clock will cost more than a similar taller one just because it is scarcer and in greater demand.

Let's take some actual heights. A modern ceiling height was until recently by regulation a minimum of 7ft. 6in. (or the metric equivalent), but some houses are still built to the 8ft. ceiling level. A house over fifty years old will more than likely have 8ft. ceilings and houses older than that may well have even taller ceilings. If your ceilings are 8ft. you can accommodate a clock of 7ft. 10in. without the problem of being overpowered by it. Most clocks of this sort of stature have a shaped top to the hood (often a swan-neck pediment), and even if the centre finial or swan-neck top is within a couple of inches of your ceiling, the visual height perceived by your eye will be much lower, namely at the shoulder of the hood-top corner.

If the clock is flat-topped, such as a cottage thirty-hour clock, then a two-inch top to ceiling gap might well look crowded. But most flat-topped clocks are in any case not nearly as tall as this. So with a flat topped clock you might well want more than a couple of inches ceiling clearance, but this is not essential with a shaped top.

If you live in an old cottage with low ceilings then your choice of clock is very limited. The point is, however, that if you can accommodate a taller clock of a particular type rather than a shorter one of that type, it will cost you less. In essence tall clocks are generally harder to sell than shorter ones (if all other things are equal), as small clocks will go into *any* house and have a very wide market. So one very important factor when buying is to consider the tallest clock you can possibly accommodate, as that way you should get a better buy.

Arched dials have a semi-circular section above the basic square shape. Any arched dial will therefore have a case at least six inches taller than a similar square-dial one, as the case rises in some sort of shaped pediment following the arched dial. So if you must have a smaller clock, consider a square rather than an arched dial. If you insist on a really small arched dial, then you are making things doubly difficult and even more costly for yourself.

When discussing height I am naturally thinking of clocks which have not been deliberately shortened to reduce the height. This happened a great deal in the past and still does today. London pagoda-style clocks, for instance, were often notoriously tall reaching to 8ft. 6in. or more. Many have had the pagoda removed to make them stand shorter and therefore more saleable, but the balance and proportion has been destroyed in doing so. The remaining clock is classed as a 'dome top', which, in fact, in unaltered form is an uncommon style for London. So when considering the very important factor of height, it is worth looking at the top and base of the clock to check whether it has been shortened, as this is regarded as something to be avoided by a serious collector. True, you may not be a 'serious collector', yet. You might, however, one day become one and, in any case, if the day ever came when you wanted to sell your 'investment' such a factor would go considerably against you.

Thirty-hour clocks normally need considerably less height for the weight-drop than eight-day clocks, and so will often come into the shorter height range. This is one solution for someone who lives in a low-ceilinged cottage. It is possible to buy a thirty-hour standing only 6ft. high and 6ft. 6in. should allow a certain degree of choice. An eight-day clock as low as 6ft. would be very unusual and even a 6ft. 6in. limit would take some finding. Such tiny eight-day clocks will cost you a considerable premium above the price they would bring if taller. Heights below 6ft would probably not allow an eight-day run.

Tiny clocks of this nature are almost always cottage clocks or farmhouse clocks as we sometimes call them. They were made small for low ceilings and are often of cottage quality being of simple, unsophisticated style, usually flat-topped, in simple 'country' woods such as pine, oak, perhaps fruitwood and just possibly solid walnut. It is extremely unlikely that they would be in veneered walnut unless they were very early examples, when they would be into high price reaches anyway. Such clocks are unlikely to be in mahogany, as this was always an expensive wood and almost always used for clocks of taller stature to suit the rooms of grander houses. If you are looking for a miniature Chippendale style with all the fine features associated with an 8ft Lancashire Chippendale clock, then you will not find it at cottage-ceiling height. Such clocks do not exist except as outright fakes or reproductions, made up to suit the needs of buyers who

Eight-day longcase with thirteen-inch dial
made about 1790 by Thomas Dean of Leigh,
Lancashire, standing 7 ft. 4 in. Plus points: fine
bookmatched mahogany veneers, small height,
original hands, centre calendar, original finial.
Negative point: slightly stocky.

ask for the impossible. I know people who claim to have one or have seen one, but I've never yet seen one I believed to be genuine and most are quite obviously fakes, which you'll be able to recognize easily after reading Chapter 8.

If you feel you must have a small clock, say less than 7ft. 6in, my advice is to cross mahogany off your list. If you find one much less than that, then it may prove to have been shortened and/or cost you a high premium in relation to its real value. Sometimes a buyer thinking of mahogany is influenced by the colour and may be quite happy with a red oak clock, which provides the colour without the height, or necessarily the price premium.

A disadvantage with small height is that a small clock can look fat. If we imagine a 10in. thirty-hour longcase of the first quarter of the eighteenth century standing 6ft. 6in., it will be finely proportioned in relation to height. Then imagine alongside it a thirteen-inch brass-dial clock of about 1780 at the same height and it is bound to look dumpy and heavy. This is why thirteen-inch dial clocks were seldom as small as that.

If your ceilings are very tall, then, in any event, a tiny clock may look lost. On the other hand, just because you have 12ft. ceilings don't get carried away and buy a 10ft. clock. If you do and you ever move house you will find it will not go in, and when you come to try to sell it, you are back again in the commercial reality of a world which, by and large, does not want 10ft. clocks.

Size is vitally important in commercial terms, as we have seen, and more important in many cases than quality. It should not be so, but it is. The unfortunate and ironic situation is sometimes that a clock of very modest quality, but of small size and clean condition will outprice a much older clock of far higher quality, merely because one is small and the other is tall.

I had an example of this just recently whereby an eight-day white-dial Scottish clock in mahogany, dating from perhaps 1850 or 60, with arched dial and swan-neck pediment, standing only 6ft. 8in. sold at exactly the same price as an eight-day, brass-dial, flat-top, oak-cased clock of the *1760s* at the same height. Ten years ago I would not have bought the Scottish clock at all. It was of no great age, had no special merits about dial or movement, but the case *was* tiny, *was* a swan-neck, *was* in mahogany and was in very clean condition. The brass-dial clock was much older, its movement far better made and was more 'desirable' in many ways. In all horological and historical terms the brass dial was a better clock, and, if there were any justice, should have been more valuable. But in the commercial world demand and taste outrates age or other factors. The mahogany clock sold not only for the same price but sold considerably quicker than the brass one. This is the sort of situation that makes a nonsense of true values, but is simply a question of commercial reality.

A buyer who could discriminate between the good and the mediocre, who had adequate ceiling height, and who was not obsessed by unnaturally small size (for the brass-dial clock was not itself a large clock, but only *looked* larger being flat-topped against the same height in a swan-neck) would have been able to select the 'better' of the two.

I recognized it as better and any clock collector would recognize it as such. I explained this to the buyer, but he still chose the mahogany. So too would many people to whom height and showy appearance meant more than quality or age. There is every likelihood that this trend will continue. Therefore in commercial terms the lesser of the two clocks is ironically the 'better', in as far as being the more saleable and probably the one to increase more rapidly in price, thus making it the better 'investment' too.

Shape, style and proportion are very important too in combining to make up a clock's price. Generally speaking, slim beats fat from many viewpoints. Older clocks, as we know, usually have smaller dials, so the slimmer cases will very often also be the older ones, though not always. In the end the matter of proportion may be one of personal preference, and it is what you like that matters most. Although you should bear in mind that the commercial world, the present-day taste is for slender lines. These things change over the years, however. If you look at a painting by Rubens, you'll see amply proportioned figures rather than the reverse. Victorian clock buyers also liked to think big. It's all a matter of the fashion of the day, and I don't see the taste for wide clocks returning just yet. If you do like large Victorian clocks, however, you'll probably get a very good buy because of their unpopularity.

I can't attempt to define what constitutes graceful shape and style against what does not. In any case I am not an arbiter on such things, and other dealers and buyers may think differently. The illustrations in this book will, however, attempt to identify what I think is and isn't good style.

Quality too means different things to different people and in different situations. For example, a high quality clockcase might be one using costly materials, or finely made using bookmatched veneers in quartered patterns. It might have a lot of blind fretting, dentil moulds and complicated, ornate and sophisticated features, which were both time consuming as well as costly to make. Quality usually means sophistication. Sometimes the word quality is used by people trying to describe what might be a very simple style of case such as an oak cottage clockcase, but a well-made example which has survived well over the years without any signs of warping, splitting, shrinkage or loose joints. In these instances it would be better if they described it as being in good condition or, as the trade often say, in 'clean' condition, because such cases are often so simple in design that it is difficult to see how they can be discussed in terms of quality. At the same time, the wood may have been very carefully selected, as with quarter-cut oak, so the materials themselves could have been chosen for their quality when cheaper would have sufficed.

With bracket clocks as well as with longcases, smaller size adds a price premium. This is also the case with spring-driven wall clocks where an eight-inch would bring much more than a similar twelve-inch.

Age is obviously important. Many longcase clocks which are two hundred years old and a little more are still surviving. Once you get back to about 1760 and beyond, however, it becomes increasingly more difficult to find a clean example for every ten years beyond this date. Therefore the price factor rises considerably with every extra ten years of age before about 1760. If you find 1780 just as excitingly old as 1720, there is no point in your paying the extra premium for the extra age you don't especially care about.

Sound condition is very important, especially in casework. There is all the difference in the world between a clock which has survived in very good condition and one which has had bumps and knocks and chips off every corner. Even though such things can be repaired, original condition counts a great deal more.

Sometimes a clock, which is otherwise very handsome, has some unpopular features. For example round dials are generally not liked. In this respect we exclude regulators, which usually have round dials. Nineteenth-century round dials are less popular than eighteenth-century ones, even though the quality of casework might be very fine. Round dials seldom blend satisfactorily in style with the square or swan-necked hood, so some have a rounded hood-top, such as the Scottish 'drumhead' style, but this is even less popular. Therefore you might well come across a Scottish drumhead longcase in the finest mahogany at half the price or less of a conventional mahogany clock of the day.

Some Scottish clocks have an even more bizarre style, such as those with a rounded trunk in tapering, fluted form, sometimes known as the tree-trunk type. With such clocks you certainly can get a low-priced buy because most people don't like them.

Certain dial features too can drastically depress the price, even to the point of rejection. Arabic hour numerals are generally less

Very fine eight-day clock by John Whitehurst of
Derby, dated 1761. All-mahogany case about
7 ft. 8 in. Plus points: exceptional maker,
mahogany is finely figured and bookmatched
to the base, original hands.

popular than Roman, especially Romans of the first white-dial period, which have dotted minutes with numbering every fifth minute. Crudely painted corner decorations can be depressing factors, whatever the theme. Some themes are definite non-starters in commercial terms. I saw a magnificent clock once with religious corner paintings and in the arch a scene of some Old Testament character slitting his son's throat as a sacrifice to the Lord. No matter how fine the casework, such themes are not bestsellers today as few people want to look at biblical scenes. Paintings of Moses receiving the tablets or of the Last Supper may have been fine in the 1840s, and many clocks of that time have them, but in today's market they are bad news commercially.

Some dial themes are ever popular. Flowers, for example, offend few people. Birds may look pretty, but many people believe in the old superstition that birds in the house bring bad luck, and some will, therefore, not consider a dial depicting birds. Some dials of the first decade of the nineteenth century have large conch shells in the corners. If these are neatly painted, then this is fine, but some look like a big yellow slug and are definitely not popular. Well-built shepherdesses and hefty female representations of Britannia don't appeal to everyone. With some of these Victorian painted scenes it may not be just the poor quality that is off-putting, but the actual subject matter itself.

Occasionally a longcase clock may have a painting including 'rolling eyes'. This is a portrait (commonly a lion) with two cut-out holes for eyes, behind which a disc sways to and fro with the pendulum to give the impression that the eyes roll. This is a novelty idea which might seem amusing, but it can be quite eerie to live with. Eccentric features such as this one may well appeal to some buyers, but may totally put off others. In commercial terms, they are less safe than the conventional.

Any comments about prices can only be very vague and there are bound to be exceptions, perhaps below, but more likely well above the figures suggested. They also exclude any factors which are eccentric or totally negative, because a clock with negative aspects will obviously fall well below one without. The problem for the novice is that he may not recognize negative aspects when he sees them.

Restoration of a longcase clock in terms of merely cleaning, refurbishing and minor casework repairs can run anywhere from £300 to double that. A clock bought in unrestored condition will therefore cost at least that amount less than a price given assuming first-class restoration had already been done.

Thirty-hour (genuine) brass dial clocks can be bought anywhere between about £800 and £2,000. Above that price one would expect there to be some special reason, such as uncommonly great age, unusual features or a special maker. Thirty-hour painted-dial clocks can be bought for as little as £250 for a late Victorian type of low quality and perhaps heavy proportions, to perhaps £2,000 at the upper end of high-quality eighteenth-century work. If the clock was above £2,000 one would expect there to be a good reason for this, and I don't think I've yet seen one above £3,000.

Eight-day longcase clocks, principally large Victorian clocks, can be bought today in auction from about £500 upwards. There is no upper limit. Having said that, once one passes the region of about £3,000 in white dials and £4,000 in brass dials, there is likely to be something outstanding pushing it into higher reaches, i.e. the kind of special aspects mentioned elsewhere in this book.

It is possible to buy a fusee English bracket clock from about £500, but at that sort of price level it is unlikely to be anything very desirable. Few good ones in restored order will be found under £2,000, but of course it all depends what we mean by 'good'.

In the end prices can only be learned by looking and comparing. After all, it is the looking and the joys of the quest which are one of the most compelling aspects of antique clocks.

11   Restoring, Setting Up and Looking After Your Clock

The question of restoration is open to all kinds of interpretation. Most people would agree that the movement of a clock needs to be cleaned thoroughly and professionally every few years. Once in twenty years is probably often enough for a clock whose movement is not exposed to the open air and dust, such as a longcase. Cleaning an antique clock usually means dismantling the whole thing, cleaning all parts, bushing to take up wear, re-assembling and testing. Most restorers give a guarantee on finished work for perhaps a year.

Some so-called restorers tie the movement to a piece of string, dip it into a pot of paraffin and haul it out to dry, perhaps making it run by tying on a heavy weight without a pendulum so that the wheels are forced to rattle around. This way they can 'thrash it into shape'. This is not approved practice and not recommended. If you take your clock to a restorer, try to find one who is recommended to you, or ask to see examples of his work first. Some restorers belong to the British Horological Institute, whose tests they have to pass in order to use the letters FBHI after their names.

It is when it comes to the dial that opinions sometimes differ. Do you leave the dial in its dirty state or do you clean it? There are opposing views about this. To clean a brass dial and re-silver the appropriate areas makes the clock look the way it was intended to look by its maker, and that is the view taken by most restorers and most clock dealers. The dirt on the dial before cleaning is not 'original', nor probably is any trace of the silvering that remains. A clock will have been cleaned several times during its life and the traces of silvering still showing are probably just the remains from the last time it was silvered, which might be only thirty or forty years ago. Silvering goes off as the lacquer covering it deteriorates, and will seldom last more than thirty years. Once it gets shabby, owners try to polish the dial with metal polish, and thus remove all remaining traces of silver as well as filling every crevice with dried polish. So, removing dirt is not removing anything that was original, nor is it akin to stripping down a wooden clock case, where that patinated surface might be an asset. There is after all no merit in dirt. So cleaning in this way is accepted practice with a brass dial clock.

On the other hand, there are people, and I can to some extent see their point of view, who feel that a clock loses some of its 'age' by cleaning its dial, in the sense that it no longer looks old. Most people would agree that it is not correct to equate dirt with age. At the same time, the brass dial of a cottage longcase clock, well-polished by its owners over the years, may have a warm charm about it which is not the same after cleaning professionally. In the end, you must decide for yourself which appearance you prefer, and if you decide you like the dial dirty, then you can always have it restored at a later date, if you wish.

Painted dials are even more subject to debate in this respect. Again then, it may be claimed there is no merit in dirt. Many white dials are grubby, covered in a 200-year-old layer of firesmoke and nicotine with a yellow, discoloured varnish. Sometimes owners have got out a wet kitchen cloth and some kitchen cleaner and wiped the dial over to remove some of the dirt, and have often removed half the thinner lettering and numbering too. The blackwork on a painted dial is a thin paint, almost as thin as Indian ink, and can quite easily be inadvertently wiped away. Most restorers and dealers will have their white dials cleaned and the worn or faded lettering replaced by going over the original outlines. Good dial restorers can do a marvellous job, but sometimes people try to do it who haven't the skill, and the result can be trembly, spidery lettering which looks pretty horrible. Good restorers can also repair any flaking, chipped, or scratched areas, matching in colour work, very much like restoring an old and dirty oil painting which is after all what the dial corners and arch decorations are. Such restoration is considered normal and acceptable in an attempt to clean the dial without changing it from the way it looked when first made. It is not considered correct to paint out the background and start again with a Dulux white ground. A badly-flaking dial may have to have some of the ground re-painted but this can be done sympathetically with the colour matched in carefully to the rest. If, however, you feel you would rather not touch the white dial of your clock, then that is up to you.

Collectors tend to accept that restoration of most clocks is necessary and normal. Lantern clocks are a bit of an exception in that some collectors and some dealers like to leave well alone. Mechanical parts certainly have to be cleaned, that is all bearing surfaces. But some dealers avoid polishing any work that shows, and some even avoid polishing the external case and dial. One reason for this is that lantern clocks have been and still are much subject to faking and alteration which is hardly surprising considering that some can be over 300 years old. A brightly polished lantern clock is much more difficult to assess in terms of originality, even for experts, as polishing can help conceal the different colour of a replaced part. Some dealers who do polish the external parts, for instance, may take photographs of it before cleaning, so that the buyer can see 'before 'as well as 'after'! If you are buying a clock from a dealer, you should ask him questions about any restoration which the clock may have had done to it, so that he can explain it to you in full if need be.

There is no shame in a replacement part of any old clock, as wear takes its toll and breakages do occur sometimes. So if a clock has a wheel or pinion or two replaced, that is rarely considered to be of any great detriment. If its wheelwork and pinions are entirely original, then clearly that is better. It is usually possible to distinguish one from the other, though a present-day restorer may match up his replacement part so skilfully that it can be hard to see the difference. In the past, restorers concentrated on mending rather than matching up and an old repair may be very well done, but can often be quite obvious.

Restoration of casework is obviously essential at times. Missing parts are normally replaced. Parts that commonly suffer from damage are the feet of clocks, whether bracket feet or plinths, since they have been long in contact with damp floors. Often clocks have been dragged from one position to another rather than carried, so that already weakened feet become broken, and these were then often removed as it was quicker and cheaper than repairing them. So many clocks today stand flat on the floor on their bases, and most dealers will restore these by fitting new feet or a new plinth, according to the judgement of the individual as to what was there originally.

So replacement feet are common and, as long as they are in keeping with the general style of the clock, they are acceptable. I can't imagine anyone refusing to buy a clock purely because the feet were replaced. Old replacements may have blended in by now anyway, so sometimes a 200-year-old clock may have 100-year-old feet, which go unnoticed as they are presumed to be original.

Less acceptable is a replaced base, i.e. the part from the bottom of the trunk to the ground. In most clocks that might put off a serious buyer. With clocks of extreme age (for their type), however, or clocks of softwood, such as pine or walnut on to pine, there is a much higher possibility of the base having been

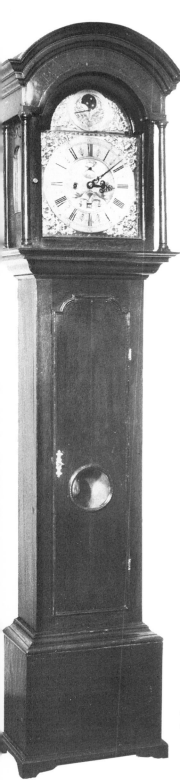

A fine eight-day clock of about 1710 by an unrecorded maker, Thomas Clark of Warrington. Twelve-inch dial. Plus points: fine engraving, penny moon in arch, herringbone edging, fine hour hand.

The oak case of the Thomas Clark of Warrington clock stands just 7 ft. 1 in.

replaced than with harder woods or younger clocks. So with clocks such as this, one may well be inclined to accept a replaced base, especially if there is something of special interest or merit about the clock anyway.

Most people who buy a clock, experienced or novices, do fully accept that anything which has survived 200 or 300 years is quite likely to have had repairs and restorations at some time in its life. We would all like to think that we could own something which is 100% original, but that possibility is becoming increasingly unlikely. As time goes by we are going to have to lower our sights even more because we are simply scraping the bottom of the barrel. There just are not enough clocks to go round. Most buyers don't mind repairs, particularly if the vendor points them out. After all there is no shame in a repair.

On the other hand, I was talking to a furniture dealer recently about this very subject – one who took a very different view. 'Take that chair,' he said. 'If you tell a customer it has three new legs, a partly replaced back and half a new seat, then you're quite simply not going to sell that chair. There's nothing more certain than that.' So the best advice to a buyer is to ask what repairs, if any, have been done, because the information may not always be volunteered.

Restoration often includes repolishing either part of a case or all of it. Sometimes the polish has suffered with age to the extent where this is unavoidable. Repolishing can be done by a good restorer in such an excellent manner that the new polish passes for original finish with patina.

Many clocks had finials – longcases in particular. These were usually in the form of brass balls with a spire top or eagle top and sometimes a flame (torch) type of top. Some were made of wood, covered in gesso and gilded. Many finials are today missing because some owners found them too fussy in the past and removed them. Some simply corroded away and collapsed as they had hollow ball centres. Many of the eagle type were removed, however, during the First World War as the eagle was associated with Germany and was far from popular here at that time.

So, swan-neck clocks had one finial in the centre, between the swans. Others had three. A three-set-up would consist either of three spires, two side spires with a centre eagle, or three eagles. Today modern reproductions can be bought, but it is virtually impossible to buy old originals. As in the past, some owners like them, and some don't. If your clock has finials you can't stand, take them off by all means, but do keep them safely in a drawer or somewhere in case you one day sell the clock.

Most clocks keep their original attached brasswork which include such things as pillar capitals, paterae, hinges, lock escutcheons, etc. Paterae were the discs decorating the swan-neck terminals and, being mostly hollow, were often polished so much by fastidious owners that they disintegrated. Modern replacements can be bought and those clocks which have modern ones do so simply because the old ones literally wore out. Modern escutcheons sometimes replace lost or broken originals. Hinges don't often wear out or need replacing, and most longcase clocks retain their originals. Surprisingly enough hinges are something that many novices examine with great attention to try to determine originality, when ninety-nine out of every hundred are original, and even if they happened to be replacements, this would be no serious detriment. There must be some particular fascination in hinges that escapes dealers and preoccupies new buyers.

Weights and pendulums are often lost or mixed up in auctions so as a result many clocks today may have unoriginal ones, although the replacements are often quite old. It is often impossible to tell replaced old ones from originals, hence this is not a terribly important aspect and has no bearing on value really, though obviously where such items can be identified as being original, it is better. Winding keys too are not always original and the same applies.

Evidence of woodworm is likely to be present in many cases, most often in the pine parts such as the pine backboard or pine substructure below the seatboard area. Such parts were seldom polished and hardly ever waxed or dusted. The holes you see are flight holes where the beetles have flown. Old ones are black or dirty; new ones are very clean, like drill holes. The danger is that there may be infestation still within the wood which may show itself later. Some owners wax over wormholes so that any new ones which appear later will then be apparent. Some dealers do the same, often to disguise new holes as old ones using dirty wax. Treatment with any proprietary woodworm killer usually works, but it does smell for a long time after. Almost any clock of respectable age will have some sign of worm somewhere, and this is not usually anything to worry about nor should it put off a serious buyer unless, of course, the wood is so honeycombed it is crumbling to pieces. If you are terrified of woodworm, then don't buy an old clock. Woodworm in the adult form are tiny flying beetles, which fly midge-like through your house all day long without you noticing. You can always try hanging a couple of those fly-killer sachets inside the case, thus forming a small gas-chamber which will kill anything that breathes.

Setting up a clock is a very simple operation, but can be infuriatingly frustrating for someone trying it for the first time. If you buy from a dealer he will either do it for you or show you exactly how. He will also advise you on what you must or must not do to that particular clock, since liberties can be taken with some clocks that would be disastrous to others. It is advisable as a general rule always to wind the hands of any clock forward, i.e. clockwise. If you wait for each hour to strike as you do so, then you cannot do wrong, but winding the hands through the hour without allowing the clock to strike can cause grave problems with certain kinds of clocks. With a weight-driven clock, such as a longcase, it follows that you must have the weights in place before you wind the hands forward, otherwise you have no power to drive the strike.

To set up a longcase clock, first get your case where you want it and wedge it tightly up against the wall. This may mean wedging a packing piece between the backboard top and the wall to fill the gap caused by your skirting board at ground level. Many clocks have a wooden batten on the upper backboard so that this can lean against the wall. A clock that can wobble to and fro may keep stopping, so the case must be firmly positioned against the wall. Some owners like to screw them to the wall. This is not essential but if you feel happier doing this, then by all means do.

If you do plan to screw the case to the wall, however, the best thing is to let the clock run for three or four weeks first, so that you know all is levelled correctly. Then drive your screw home to hold it firm and safe from dashing children and the roving vacuum.

Setting up a longcase is all a question of levels, and what level you are measuring. You need to have some means of ensuring that you can re-level the case again if it moves or if you move it to another room or another house even. Therefore you are best to take a particular point on your case on which you can read the level with a spirit level. Set up your case, first of all, complete with hood but without its movement. I usually check the level on that section of the hood immediately in front of the glass hood door, since all clocks (virtually all) have a flat moulding projecting just there – the lowest projecting moulding of the hood itself.

When that moulding is level side to side, wedge the clock so that it leans slightly backwards against the wall. Leaning too far back will cause the pendulum to bump against the backboard and too far forward will cause the weights to bump against the door. With some shallow cases you may have to accept the latter but if so, no harm will be done. The only level which matters to you from now on is the side-to-side one on that particular moulding

Eight-day oak-cased brass-dial clock made in
the 1740s by Emanuel Hopperton of Leeds,
crossbanded in burr elm. The height is only 7 ft.
Plus factors: small height, clean condition,
quarter-cut oak.

(not the front-to-back level). In fact the clockcase should lean fractionally back to rest against the wall in a stable state. If your clock sways about, pack the case at the front feet with small wedges of hardboard till it doesn't. Once the case is levelled, any adjustment from here on will be to the clock, not the case.

With the case 'level' and firmly wedged so it can't move, take off the hood and set the movement (with its wooden seatboard) in place. With an eight-day clock, put on the *left* weight by slipping the pulley over the gutline and hanging it on. This will hold the movement safely in place during the rest of the operation. You may need two hands to do this unless you are experienced at it. If not, get someone to hold the movement stable until you get this first weight in place. Later you will learn how to hang a weight with one hand.

Try on the hood at this stage to see if you have the dial positioned centrally to the glass. If not, shuffle it till it is. Then remove the hood again and slip on the pendulum by pushing the suspension spring through the fork of the crutch and into the slit in the back-cock. Then hang on the right-hand weight. If you are not sure which weight is which, the left-hand one is usually the heaviest, as it controls the striking and this usually requires more power than is needed to simply keep the clock going. Sometimes both weights are the same size and then you have no decision to make. If you wish to be awkward try hanging on the right-hand weight first. This will make the crutch rock about and it will therefore be harder for you to get the pendulum through the fork, though it will not cause any damage. A thirty-hour clock has only one weight, so there the easiest thing is to first hang the pendulum, then the weight, for the reason just stated.

Now give the pendulum a gentle push and see what happens. If the crutch has not been bent in transit, the clock will run. If you've just bought the clock from some place where it was not already set up level and working, such as an auction, then in all likelihood the crutch is already bent out of its correct angle and the clock will not run till you put this right. If the clock stops infrequently, perhaps after a few hours, then you are probably almost there with the crutch position but not quite. If it runs for only a few minutes, the crutch is well out of position. To reset the crutch is very simple and a clockmaker can do it in seconds. If you are new to it, it may take two or three attempts, so do not worry if it does not work the first time.

A level clock 'in beat' will tick evenly from side to side like someone walking – the time lapse between ticks being about equal. A clock 'out of beat' will tick unevenly, like someone limping, and the ticks will sound alternately long and short. If you watch the pendulum bob you will probably see it swinging further over to one side than the other till the clock finally grinds to a halt. Bend the crutch rod (which is made of soft steel for this purpose, though some can be very stiff) along its length, not at the top joint or you may break it, and bend it towards the direction of the heaviest or longest tick. If the clock ticks heaviest to the right then bend the crutch to the right. You will hear the difference at once when you next push the pendulum to start the clock.

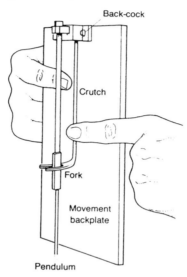

Setting a clock in beat

Setting up a weight-driven wall clock, such as a tavern clock or hooded clock, is exactly the same process, though you must ensure the case cannot swing left or right. The same principle of setting the crutch in beat also applies to a fusee wall clock, a bracket clock or indeed any other British clock.

Suppose you have got your clock home in a completely restored condition and fully working. How do you look after it? The best advice I can give is that you wind it as required, but otherwise leave it alone. Some owners are obsessed with fiddling with their clock, adjusting needlessly, dusting bits that don't get dusty and so on. These people are asking for trouble and usually find it. It is the easiest thing in the world for a duster to catch the hands of a clock unintentionally. Several times a year people arrive on my doorstep clutching a broken hand and explaining that they were 'only dusting it'.

By all means wax polish the clock case. Any kind of wax at all is better than none, since wax will feed the wood and help to prevent it drying out as well as adding an increasingly handsome glow to it. Use whatever polish you use for your other furniture. An old-fashioned mixture of beeswax and turpentine is ideal as it is what past generations of clock polishers used. You can buy it today under all kinds of brand names. If you use this, polish a small area at a time and shine it up before moving on. Do not let it dry hard as you might then find it much more of a struggle to bring to a shine. A warmed duster is helpful for the final rub over.

If you use a spray polish, and there's no reason you shouldn't, then spray the cloth, not the clock. That way you will not be likely to miss any unrubbed spots of polish which, if left to set, may well spot-mark the wood.

The dials of most clocks are contained within a reasonably dust-proof container behind glass. Resist the urge to dust the dial, although you may do it carefully once every ten years or so. By all means, clean the clock glass, but leave the dial alone. If you put anything on to a painted dial you risk removing the fine lettering. If you polish a lacquered brass dial, you will wear the lacquer through so much sooner, if not at once, and it will then go patchy and become a blotchy mess.

Many people are terrified their central heating will destroy a clock case. If you stand a longcase next to a radiator, it probably will. Position the clock somewhere sensible, and not where the sunlight can shine on to it. Hot sun will melt glue behind veneers and can ultimately cause bubbling and lifting as well as fading of the colour. It is not so much the heat of modern homes as the extreme dryness which may harm your clockcase. Most clocks have been shrinking over two centuries or more as a result of their timber drying out, and are unlikely to shrink further unless you live in intolerably hot conditions. A small basin of water placed inside a longcase (on the floor) will produce some moisture and may help. It will probably need filling once a week. If so, hopefully some of the evaporated moisture will have gone into the inside of your case.

Americans regularly ask what will happen to the clock in an earthquake. The answer is if your house collapses, it will be crushed to pieces! My best suggestion is that you get out of the house fast and leave the clock to its fate. I'm not in a position to give advice about earthquakes.

Clocks don't generally break by themselves; it is the owners who break them. Some people and clocks just don't go together and I know that they will be for ever on the phone saying: 'It's doing it again, Mr Loomes.' They regard the clock as having a will of its own, as being in charge of its own actions and destiny, when in fact a clock is only a machine. It will do what you make it

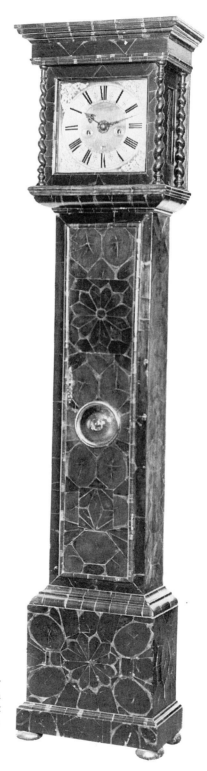

Eight-day clock of about 1700 by Henry
Simcock of Daventry. Parquetry veneering in
laburnum with oystershell pieces. Height about
6 ft. 10 in. A highly desirable clock.

do no more or no less. If certain conditions interfere with its normal running, it will stop. The clock has no other way of telling you that something is wrong. So here is a fault-finding list for the most common causes of stopping. These are not breakages, not mechanical faults, do not require the services of a repairer, but can be put right by the owner.

If the clock keeps stopping, it is important to note how long it runs between stops and at what time it stops, as these factors will give a clue to the problem.

A clock which stops at five minutes to the hour (warning time for the strike) is probably slightly out of beat. The solution is level up the case and/or adjust the crutch setting. A clock running no more than half an hour at a time is probably considerably off level or out of beat and the solution is the same. A clock running no more than a few minutes at a time is probably well off level or well out of beat and the same remedy will cure this.

If an eight-day clock runs well for four or five days but stops when the weights reach the pendulum bob and then functions correctly for the rest of the week, the problem is what is called 'five-day stopping'. The case is not wedged firmly enough to the wall or else the case joints are weak which can make the body can sway imperceptibly. The clock loses power as the swaying pendulum attracts the weights into an invisible swing through gravitational attraction, which ultimately draws the pendulum to a standstill. If you think that sounds complicated, then you would be correct and this is why we refer to it as five-day stopping for short! It could of course be four days or six, but the cause is the same. A thick carpet and underfelt can produce this effect as they act like a mini-trampoline. Wedge it tighter against the wall or, better still, screw it to the wall.

In the past many owners used to screw their clocks to the wall, as most backboards will reveal by the number of holes in them. I had an early longcase once with forty-two holes in the back from previous household fixings. Most people do not do this today, and by no means is it essential. If, however, you get this five-day stopping problem, it's perhaps the simplest way to cure it.

Stopping for none of the above reasons may be due to several possible factors, most of them involving the loss of power – either partial or total. A clock with no power getting through will run for a minute or two, or even less. Power loss means that something somewhere is trapped, thus preventing the weight pulling the wheels round. Possible reasons are:

1   On a thirty-hour clock the rope joint is too stiff and catches the escape wheel when it passes close by. Solution: weaken the

stiffness of the joint by flexing it repeatedly or rejointing it more loosely.

2   Hands catching against each other. Solution: adjust hands so that they are free to pass.

3   Calendar is out of frame and calendar drive is catching against calendar disc rather than driving it. Solution: take hands back (if possible), reposition calendar indicator to a whole number read-out and then try starting clock again.

4   Gutline (on eight-day clock) has crossed over itself on the barrel and therefore cannot turn. Solution: remove drive weight, uncross line, replace weight and restart.

5   Pendulum rubbing on backboard. Solution: pack clock backboard further forward from wall.

6   Clock has run down. Solution: rewind it. This is not as silly as it sounds as the barrel may be empty of line even though the weight is well above the ground.

7   On a thirty-hour the weight may have caught against the counterweight in its descent.

8   Weight or weights may be catching on lower door frame, thus unable to descend lower. This will be obvious by weight jolting when main door is opened to investigate. Solution: lean clock a little further back towards the wall to let weight(s) clear.

9   On eight-day clocks the tied off end of the gutline may be trapped against a tooth on mainwheel (or even any other wheel). Solution: free line end and retie more neatly out of the way.

10   On eight-days the gutline may have slipped off the barrel and be trapped between wheels. Solution: remove weight and attempt to free line. This may even involve untying the tied-off end, unthreading the whole line and rewinding from scratch. Sometimes a small screwdriver can be used to raise the wheel click gently, thus freeing the barrel so that the line can be drawn out fully before rewinding.

11   On thirty-hour clocks the rope or chain may have slipped off its ratchet wheel. Solution: slip it back on again.

12   On eight-day clocks the weight pulley may have slipped off its line, so that the line cannot run. Solution: slip pulley back on to line.

13   Rope, chain, or gutline fouling on the seatboard, perhaps against a jagged or splintered piece of board. Solution: free it and then cut the offending splinter free with a knife.

14   Weight line twisted above pulley preventing weight pulling. Solution: untwist and search for cause of twisting.

15   Seconds hand too close to dial and fouling against it. Solution: ease seconds hand away from dial slightly by pulling

(not bending). This hand fits by pushing into place. If pushed too far home, it may rub against the dial.

There may be others I cannot bring to mind, but any loss of drive power simply means following visually the drive line from the weight through its various stages to the barrel, looking out for any fouling on the way.

When moving an eight-day clock a useful tip which may save a lot of fiddling about untangling gutlines from between wheels is to wind the clock almost fully with the weights in place, till the weight pulleys come within an inch (no closer) of the seatboard. Place a three-inch strip of masking tape round the neatly coiled line on the visible side of each barrel with the tape following the curve of the barrel. Use masking tape as sellotape will not stick to gutlines as they are slightly waxy or oily. Then remove weights and remove clock movement on its seatboard.

This keeps the lines neatly coiled, avoids them tangling, criss-crossing over themselves or getting trapped between wheels. It also avoids the struggle with long lengths of uncontrollable line, which occurs when the alternative method is used, namely of releasing the barrel click and letting out the whole gutline. Don't forget to remove the tape before setting the clock in motion after assembly.

Some new owners of a clock have an irresistible obsession with oiling. I don't know what it is about clocks that brings out the urge to oil in people whose garden gate hinge won't swing for rust. Please resist the urge. Too much oil is worse than no oil at all. People grab an engineer's oil can that might well have once lubricated locomotive wheels, close their eyes and squirt oil blindly into the movement. Apart from the almighty mess when it drips down to the carpet some hours later, this is putting oil where it should never be and where none is needed. The same thing goes for those who like to spray WD40 from an aerosol under the impression that what might be good for cold-starting a car, must be good for a clock.

Oil should not be put on to the teeth of wheels or it will make a sticky surface to which dust particles will adhere, thus forming a gritty compound as the wheels rub it well in. If you need oil, it should be put very sparingly on the projecting point of each pivot.

Special clock oil can be bought, but any light oil such as sewing-machine oil will do. Engine oil, goose grease and petroleum jelly are not recommended.

Half fill a teaspoon with light oil. Take a piece of thin wire about six inches long – a piece of a wire coathanger is ideal! Dip the end into the oil to pick up a small amount. Put a pinheadful outside the backplate where each arbor protrudes. Then do the same inside the backplate, and on both sides of the frontplate. This means you have four oiling points per arbor. Do it for each arbor on the going and strike trains (and on the third train if there is one). These parts cannot be reached other than with a thin wire, so an oilcan is useless and in any case too generous. Putting too much oil on is pointless as it will simply trickle down the plates.

Some old books mention oiling with a feather, which sounds like as good a way as any of making a mess. What this probably meant was to use a goose quill (like a quill pen) applying oil on the pointed end, not the feathery bit.

I've heard of people who place a saucer of paraffin on the floor inside a longcase clock. What they imagine it will do I have no idea, but it won't do anything for the clock. If you like the smell of paraffin, then fine. Otherwise oil it in the same way that most people do.

Some people used to place an old pillow on the floor inside a longcase clock to prevent a falling weight crashing through the base of the case or the floorboards when the gutline snapped. Terrifying things can breed in old pillows inside clockcases, and it is far simpler to keep an eye on your gutlines for any fraying. New gutlines will last twenty years or so unless maltreated, and new lines are very cheap. Never put old lines back on to a clean clock and then you can save the pillows for the bed.

While dealing with superstitious practices, let's clarify the point that if your clock strikes thirteen it is not the work of the devil. A countwheel-striking clock may well strike twelve followed by one, hence the mysterious thirteen which was caused by the clock failing to lock off after twelve. Call in a clock doctor not a priest.

Conversion Chart

Clock dials and cases were built using feet and inches as the measuring system of the day. Certain *avant-garde* auctioneers today try to drag us all kicking and screaming into the world of metrics, which is meaningless to anyone who, like me, is over the age of 25. They describe dials and cases in metric measurements, though some of the kinder ones use double measurements. I cannot begin to form a mental picture of an item with a listed height of 217cm. So for the benefit of those, like myself, the following chart of relative measurements might help.

6 in.	dial approximately equals	15 cm.
10 in.		25.5 cm.
11 in.		28 cm.
12 in.		30.5 cm.
13 in.		33 cm.
14 in.		38 cm.
6 ft.		183 cm.
6 ft. 3in.		190 cm.
6 ft. 6in.		198 cm.
6 ft. 9in.		206 cm.
7 ft.		213 cm.
7 ft. 3in.		221 cm.
7 ft. 6in.		229 cm.
7 ft. 9in.		236 cm.
8 ft.		244 cm.
8 ft. 3in.		252 cm.
8 ft. 6in.		259 cm.
9 ft.		274 cm.

Bibliography

Books

Allan, Charles, *Old Stirling Clockmakers* (*including St. Ninians*) pub. privately, Stirling, 1990)

Baillie, G.H., *Watchmakers and Clockmakers of the World, vol.1.* (NAG Press, 1976) (see also Loomes)

Barder, R.C.R., *English Country Grandfather Clocks* (David & Charles, 1983)

Barker, D., *The Arthur Negus Guide to Clocks* (Hamlyn, 1980)

Bates, Keith, *Clockmakers of Northumberland & Durham* (Pendulum Publications, 1980)

Beeson, C.F.C., *Clockmaking in Oxfordshire* (Museum of the History of Science, 1989)

Bellchambers, J.K., *Somerset Clockmakers* (Antiquarian Horological Society)

——*Devonshire Clockmakers* (The Devonshire Press Ltd, 1962)

Britten, F.J., *Old Clocks and Watches and Their Makers* (Methuen, 9th ed., 1982)

Brown, H.M., *Cornish Clocks & Clockmakers* (David & Charles, 1970)

Bruton, Eric., *The Longcase Clock* (Hart-Davis, 1970)

——*The Wetherfield Collection of Clocks* (NAG Press, 1981)

Daniel, John, *Leicestershire Clockmakers* (Leicestershire Museums, 1975)

Dawson, P., Drover, C.B. and Parkes, D.W., *Early English Clocks* (Antique Collectors' Club, 1982)

Dowler, Graham, *Gloucestershire Clock & Watchmakers* (Phillimore, 1984)

Edwardes, E.L., *The Grandfather Clock* (Sherrat, 1980)

——*The Story of the Pendulum Clock* (Sherrat, 1977)

Elliott, D.J., *Shropshire Clocks & Clockmakers* (Phillimore, 1979)

Haggar, A.L., & Miller, L.F., *Suffolk Clocks & Clockmakers* (Antiquarian Horological Society, 1974)

Hana, W.F.J., *English Lantern Clocks* (Blandford Press, 1979)

Hudson, Felix., *Scottish Clockmakers* (F. Hudson, Dunfermline (1982)

Hughes, R.G., *Derbyshire Clock & Watch Makers* (Derby Museum, 1976)

Lee, R.A., *The Knibb Family Clockmakers* (Manor House Publications, 1963)

Legg, Edward, *Clock & Watchmakers of Buckinghamshire* (Bradwell Abbey Field Centre, 1976)

Lloyd, H. Alan, *Old Clocks* (Benn, 1958)

Loomes, Brian, *Complete British Clocks* (David & Charles, 1978)

——*Country Clocks & their London Origins* (David & Charles, 1976)

——*The Early Clockmakers of Great Britain* (NAG Press, 1982)

——*Grandfather Clocks & their Cases* (David & Charles, 1985)

——*Lancashire Clocks & Clockmakers* (David & Charles, 1975)

——*Watchmakers & Clockmakers of the World, vol.2.* (NAG Press, 1976, revised 1989)

——*Westmorland Clocks & Clockmakers* (David & Charles, 1974)

——*White Dial Clocks: The Complete Guide* (David & Charles, 1981)

Loomes, Brian, *Yorkshire Clockmakers* (revised edition) (George Kelsall, 1985)
Lyle Official Antiques Review, The (Lyle Publications)
McKenna Joseph, *Watch & Clockmakers of Warwickshire* (Pendulum Press, 1985)
——*Watch & Clockmakers of Birmingham* (Pendulum Press, 1986)
Mason, Bernard, *Clock & Watch Making in Colchester* (Country Life, 1969)
Mather, H., *Clock & Watchmakers of Nottinghamshire* (The Friends of Nottingham
    Museum, 1979)
Miller's Antiques Price Guide (Miller's Publications Ltd)
Moore, Nicholas, *Chester Clocks & Clockmakers* (Chester Museum, 1970s)
Norgate, J & M., & Hudson, F. *Dunfermline Clockmakers* (F. Hudson, 1982)
Peate, I., *Clock & Watch Makers in Wales* (Welsh Folk Museum, 1960)
Penfold, John, *The Clockmakers of Cumberland* (Brant Wright Associates, 1977)
Penman, L., *The Clock Repairer's Handbook* (David & Charles/Arco, 1985)
Ponsford, Clive N., *Devon Clocks & Clockmakers* (David & Charles, 1985)
——*Time in Exeter* (Headwell Vale Books, 1978)
——Authers, W.P., *Clocks & Clockmakers of Tiverton* (W.P. Authers, 1977)
Pryce, W.T.R., & Davies. T. Alun., *Samuel Roberts, Clockmaker* (Welsh Folk
    Museum, 1985)
Robinson, T., *The Longcase Clock* (Antique Collectors' Club, 1981)
Rose, Ronald, E., *English Dial Clocks* (Antique Collectors' Club, 1978)
Royer-Collard, F.B., *Skeleton Clocks* (NAG Press, 1969)
Seaby, W.A., *Clockmakers of Warwick & Leamington* (Warwick Museum, 1981)
Smith, E., *Striking and Chiming Clocks* (David & Charles/Arco, 1985)
Smith, John, *Old Scottish Clockmakers* (E.P. Publishing Ltd., 1975)
Snell, Michael, *Clocks & Clockmakers of Salisbury* (Hobnob Press, 1986)
Symonds, R.W., *Thomas Tompion his Life & Work* (Spring Books, 1968)
Tebbutt, Laurence, *Stamford Clocks and Watches* (Dolby Bros Ltd., 1975)
Treherne, A.A., *Nantwich Clockmakers* (Nantwich Museum, (1986)
Tribe, T. &. Whatmoor, P., *Dorset Clocks & Clockmakers* (Tanat Books, 1981)
Tyler, E.J., *Clock Types* (Longman, 1982)
——*The Clockmakers of Sussex* (Watch & Clock Book Society, 1986)
Vernon, J., *The Grandfather Clock Maintenance Manual* (David & Charles/Van
    Nostrand Rheinhold, 1983)
Walker, J.E.S., *Hull & East Riding Clocks* (Hornsea Museum Publications, 1982)
Wallace, William, *Time in Hamilton* (1981).
White, George, *English Lantern Clocks* (Antique Collectors' Club, 1989)

Periodicals

Antiquarian Horology
Antiquarian Horological Society
New House
High Street
Ticehurst
Wadhurst
East Sussex TN5 7AL

Clocks Magazine
Argus Specialist Publications
Argus House
Boundary Way
Hemel Hempstead
Herts HP2 7ST

Horological Journal
British Horological Institute
Upton Hall
Newark
Notts. NG23 5TE

The Bulletin
National Association of Watch & Clock
    Collectors
P.O. Box 33
Columbia
Pennsylvania 17512
USA

Index

Index